WHITE HOUSE: CONFIDENTIAL

Second Edition, Revised and Expanded

WHITE HOUSE: CONFIDENTIAL

THE LITTLE BOOK OF WEIRD PRESIDENTIAL HISTORY

GREGG STEBBEN AND AUSTIN HILL

Foreword by Congressman Joseph Crowley

CUMBERLAND HOUSE
NASHVILLE, TENNESSEE

WHITE HOUSE: CONFIDENTIAL
PUBLISHED BY CUMBERLAND HOUSE PUBLISHING
431 Harding Industrial Drive
Nashville, Tennessee 37211

Cover design: Gore Studio, Inc.
Book design: Mary Sanford

Library of Congress Cataloging-in-Publication Data
Stebben, Gregg.
  White House confidential : the little book of weird presidential history / Gregg Stebben and Austin Hill. — [2nd ed., rev. and expanded].
     p. cm.
  ISBN-13: 978-1-58182-544-2 (pbk. : alk. paper)
  ISBN-10: 1-58182-544-7 (pbk. : alk. paper)
  1. Presidents—United States—History—Miscellanea. 2. Presidents—United States—Biography—Miscellanea. I. Hill, Austin, 1964– II. Title.
  E176.1.S7 2006
  973.09'9—dc22

                                                                    2006017601

Printed in Canada
1 2 3 4 5 6 7—12 11 10 09 08 07 06

For our mothers, Arlene and Loisann:

You may not have raised us to be presidents . . .
but you did at least teach us right from wrong.

And for our wives, Jody and Nell,

who taught us all the rest.

CONTENTS

FOREWORD

It is easy to forget, especially in the age of the 24-hour news cycle, that the concept of the White House being a haven for complex, larger-than-life personas is not entirely endemic to our age. Since our nation's birth, as Gregg Stebben and Austin Hill show in this wonderful book, a multitude of individuals whose personalities have loomed large have always been holding the highest office in the land.

It may also come as a surprise that these individuals, who led the country through unique eras, wars, and historical epochs, were often engaged in the same types of scandals, personal issues, affairs, power struggles, and bitter rivalries that play out in our newspapers, television news shows, and Internet blogs of today.

True, in our digital multimedia age, where the lines between public figures and celebrity are often blurred, the American public has come to expect politicians to be treated with the same dripping sensationalism thought to be reserved only for Hollywood stars. It could be even argued that presidents, presidential candidates, and maybe our political culture as a whole embraces and fosters this superficial glossing over of Constitutional power.

After all, it would seem foolish for those vying for the top spot of the U.S. government to turn down a television spot for the chance to talk about their family vacations with Jay Leno or David Letterman, or to forego an interview with Oprah Winfrey. These publicity opportunities are sought by present-day politicians not just to spill their guts but to remind their public that hey, after all, they are only human too.

We may be fooled into thinking past American presidents had more scruples, or at least led sanctimonious lives—or just very dull ones. Perhaps they filled their schedules and time with only momentous events such as political showdowns with Congress and leading the nation in war. Or that their time was largely taken up by the ceremonial hum-drum of cabinet meetings and treaty signings. But as readers will discover in the pages of *White House: Confidential,* such thinking is dead wrong.

Strange, salacious, and sometimes shocking factoids about our nation's past presidents are chronicled in this book, and delivered through gossipy tabloid sensibilities of our age. Money scandals, sexual affairs, sibling liabilities, and downright bizarre behavior are fair game for the authors, who feel no shame in providing all the juicy details, often drawing interesting parallels and comparisons between past and present.

Where else would we discover that Richard Nixon, who was a successful debater on his high school's debate team, probably also learned a thing or two about stump speaking during his stint as a carnival barker? Or that Ronald Reagan was actually considered to play Rick in the classic film *Casablanca*? Or that Gerald Ford was a male model and appeared on the cover of *Cosmopolitan* magazine in the 1930s? Or that Harry Truman opened a gentle-men's fine clothing store in Kansas City, which went broke three years later?

This book is a reminder—to history buff and novice alike—that the top residents of the White House are, and have always been, a fascinating bunch with tales to tell.

It is especially interesting how the book goes beyond just presenting a lineup of some of the juiciest tidbits of presidential lore (though most are in here) by exploring some interesting hypothetical questions about American history. Reading about what mistakes and misjudgments committed by Presidents George Washington through Lyndon Baines Johnson a blogging news media would have made hay of is really fascinating.

Through tales that will raise eyebrows, incite laughter, and even elicit the occasional gasp, Gregg Stebben and Austin Hill strike the right tone of scholarly attention to detail and fun in elaborating on the complicated and fascinating lives of the occupants of the White House.

Leafing through this wonderful and fun book, one discovers there are so many interest-ing and delicious facts about the presidency that are not widely known and seldom men-tioned—maybe for good reason—until now.

—Joseph Crowley
Member of Congress, D-New York

INTRODUCTION

President of the United States. What a rotten job.

You're the guy or gal who's always to blame. The economy. Foreign policy. Drugs in the schools. Crime on the streets. . . . It's all your fault.

Throw in the official duties: commander in chief of the armed services and chief executive of the biggest, fattest, least efficient organization in the known world. You've got the power to nominate your good friends A, B, and C for secretary of state, Supreme Court justice, or maybe ambassador to some country called Paradíso. But you've got to do it without ticking off the general public, too many members of Congress, or your good friends X, Y, and Z (who thought they were going to get the jobs because that's what you said you were going to do). You also get the power to declare war. (Sort of.) But what if you do it and in retrospect realize you were just having a bad day? And on top of all that you've got to decide whether you should sign or veto a bunch of bills from Congress—and every time you try to read one you fall fast asleep.

All of which causes you to wonder: Does anyone—other than your press secretary, a handful of radio call-in talk show hosts (like one of the coauthors of this very book, Austin Hill), and a couple of other people with political futures at stake—really care about any of this stuff?

Somehow you get the sense that what the American public really expects from you, their president, is entertainment. Giant, screaming headlines full of corruption, scandal, sex, stupidity, sleaze. And presumably they want that sex, stupidity, and sleaze to be yours. After all, you've finally made it. You're in the center ring. You're president of the United States—the all-star attraction. And now it's you everyone wants as the fall guy.

This of course means that it's also your job to collaborate with the media to destroy your life, your reputation, your family—and your knees (a reference to tumbling, tumbling

Gerald Ford and Bill Clinton, as well as to Thomas Jefferson, who once took a spill while showing off for his married girlfriend), all in an effort to entertain the American people.

Thus far, our legion of presidents has lived up to the challenge. And when there's been nothing true to report, the media has been only too happy to help out; in the absence of truth they report on rumor, innuendo, a thread of a thread of a story heard somehow, somewhere.

Are we, the people, really this callous? Petty? Shallow? Or easily amused?

Probably not.

The truth is most of us would rather have a straight-shooting, stand-up kind of president than one who's a buffoon or a scoundrel or a cheat. In fact, what most of us really want is a president who's a hero. Or a saint. Someone with impeccable moral values and judgment. A flawless personal history. The sort of guy or gal who has never made an enemy or, barring that, the sort who has made many—but for all the right, fight-for-what-you-believe-in reasons.

Yup. This is what we desperately crave, even though it's a standard we ourselves could never hope to live up to. So we take what we can get, and then we act horrified when our presidents and presidential candidates do the same dirty, rotten stuff with their lives we do with ours.

And now that you've spent the last few moments imagining the job was yours, aren't you relieved to remember it's a job that actually belongs to someone else?

A COUPLE OF SMALL DISCLAIMERS

I. Your authors, too, are members of the media. Therefore we want to fulfill our obligation to you, the reader, by entertaining you with stories about the presidents based either on the stupid, rotten stuff they've actually done or at least the stupid, rotten stuff of which they've been publically accused. However, we want to do this without creating a scandal of our own. For that reason we state up front that this work contains absolutely no groundbreaking or earth-shattering new research on the behavior of presidents past or present. Furthermore, we make absolutely no warrants toward the truth or veracity of any of the information contained in this book.

   This much you can count on, however: If it appears here, regardless of how cruel, mean, baseless, or untrue it may be, someone somewhere (other than your authors) reported it first.

II. Much of what you read in this book is funny today, but it wasn't very funny when it happened. Why not? For the same reason you're probably not laughing about Watergate or Contragate or Whitewater or the aftermath of the current President Bush's unsuccessful search for weapons of mass destruction (WMDs) in Iraq. History is rarely entertaining for those who are deceived or wronged or maligned or misled or screwed in the course of the history-making process. For this reason, you'll find many more juicy tidbits about presidents of the first hundred and seventy or so years of our history than about our past five or six commanders in chief. After all, we're the ones who have to ante up for their follies, and that's no laughing matter.

WHITE HOUSE: CONFIDENTIAL

1

Weird Family Values!

HOW'S THIS FOR weird:

> Franklin Delano *Roosevelt* married his fifth cousin,
> Eleanor *Roosevelt.* At the wedding Eleanor was given
> away by her uncle—Theodore *Roosevelt,* president of
> the United States.
>
> For FDR and Eleanor, though . . .

THIS WAS JUST the beginning of a lifetime of weirdness that involved mistresses, lesbians, and live-in lovers right there at the White House!

Most people would agree that the best way to avoid getting caught when having an affair is to have it with someone your spouse doesn't know. Guess no one told FDR that—his first mistress was Lucy Mercer, Eleanor's social secretary.

When Eleanor found out FDR was having an affair, she offered to let him out of their marriage. But FDR didn't take her up on it; he knew Lucy, being Catholic, would never marry a man who was divorced. Oh, and there might have been one other small reason why FDR didn't want to divorce Eleanor: He knew that if he did, his mother would cut him off from the family fortune.

After he and Lucy got caught, FDR had to find a new mistress. *Hey, I've got a great idea!* he might have thought to himself, *Maybe I'll go look for one down in the secretarial pool!* But you can't say he didn't learn from experience—instead of having an affair with Mrs. Roosevelt's new secretary, he had his next affair with a new secretary of his own.

Her name was Missy LeHand, and everyone in the Roosevelt family—Eleanor and all six kids—knew about the relationship. Of course, it would have been impossible for them not to know—Missy was living with the president right there at the White House.

Obviously the president and Missy had to show some decorum. That's why Missy had her own set of rooms—a living room, bedroom, and bath—at the White House, although she could frequently be seen sitting on the president's lap in the Oval Office at night or in her bathrobe in the president's own suite. Lady that she was, however, she was always gone by breakfast.

In the meantime, Eleanor embarked on a strange, "secret" life of her own that first involved a rough-hewn, cigar-

Lovers? Or just very good friends?

Some have said that Eleanor's attachment to strong women like Lorena Hickok was emotional but not physical. Following is a letter Eleanor sent to Hick in 1933—you be the judge:

Good-night, dear one. I want to put my arms around you and kiss you at the corner of your mouth. And in a little more than a week now—I shall.

chomping reporter from the Associated Press. Lorena Hickok was her name, and she and Eleanor were lovers (spiritually, if not physically) for more than ten years.

Eleanor and "Hick," as Lorena was often called, had their own bizarre living arrangements at the White House. The two women had separate rooms across the West Hall and could often be seen running back and forth from one another's quarters.

Eleanor was a good sport about FDR's living arrangements with Missy—after all, it had been going on since he was governor of New York. On the other hand, the president wasn't so crazy about having Hick hanging around. One day, he stormed through the White House yelling, "I want that woman kept out of this house!" From that point on, the White House maids and Eleanor did everything they could to keep the president and Hick apart.

The weird story of the Roosevelts has many endings, by the way—but not all of them are happy:

- While living at the White House with Eleanor, Lorena Hickok fell in love with another woman and moved out.
- Missy LeHand suffered a cerebral hemorrhage, had to be hospitalized, and then died.
- Shortly after Missy fell ill, the husband of FDR's old flame, Lucy Mercer, had a devastating stroke, so she and FDR "took up" again.
- It was Lucy Mercer, not Eleanor, who was with FDR when he died of a stroke in 1945.

Oh, Happy Day!

FDR's first Inauguration Day, that is. And why shouldn't it have been happy? After all, FDR knew his wife would be there. And he knew that his lover, Missy LeHand, would be there. And he knew (but kept it secret from both Eleanor and Missy) that his former lover, Lucy, would be there too. Not that Eleanor would have noticed— after all, she spent the night before the inauguration at a hotel with Hick and, like a young schoolgirl in love, wore Hick's sapphire ring on her finger as she attended the festivities of the day.

WEIRD FAMILY VALUES!

Did FDR treat his dog better than his wife?

Fala was a little Scotch terrier FDR took with him everywhere (although he certainly didn't extend the same invitation to Eleanor). To the press and public Fala was known as "The Informer" because wherever FDR traveled—even if his plans were secret because of the war—Fala had to be walked at every train stop and thus gave the president's "secret" presence away.

- Perhaps in these cases, money speaks louder than words. When FDR died his estate was worth an estimated $1.9 million. He left half of that to his wife, Eleanor, and the other half to cover Missy LeHand's medical bills. There wasn't a cent left over for Lucy Mercer.

LET'S TAKE A LOOK AT ANOTHER ROOSEVELT

Teddy Roosevelt's wife, Alice, and his mother both died on the same day: January 14, 1884. His mother died of typhoid; his wife died of Bright's disease three days after giving birth to daughter Alice.

Three years later Teddy married an old childhood friend, Edith. Together they had five children.

Unlike his naughty nephew, FDR, Teddy didn't feel a need to run wild. Instead he was a devoted family man. Yet the Teddy Roosevelt White House was almost as much a zoo as FDR's White House because Teddy got great joy from indulging his children's every whim:

- Teddy allowed his kids to keep a few pets, including ten dogs named Susan, Skip, Scamp, Sailor Boy, Peter, Manchu, Allen, Gem, Jessie, and Bill; a horned toad named Bill; four guinea pigs named Bob Evans, Father Grady, Dewey Jr., and Dewey Sr.; a blue macaw named Eli Yale; Emily Spinach, a garter snake; two ponies named Algonquin and Fidelity; a badger named Josiah; two cats named Tom Quartz and Slippers; a bear named Jonathon Edward; a lion; and a one-legged rooster.
- Every member of Teddy's family owned a pair of stilts—and that included the First Lady. Edith Roosevelt was so well coordinated and so good at playing different games and sports that young Quentin once said of her, "I'll bet Mother was a boy when she was little."
- When Archie Roosevelt was sick in bed with the measles, Teddy saw nothing wrong with letting sons Kermit and Quentin sneak Algonquin the pony up the White House elevator to visit him.
- Daughter Ethel was a notorious tomboy; one of her favorite things to do was to sit on cookie sheets and slide down the White House steps.
- After daughter Alice interrupted one of his meetings at the White House one day, Teddy threw up his arms in resignation and swore, "I can be president of the United States, or I can control Alice. I cannot possibly do both."

WEIRD FAMILY VALUES!

Think President Clinton
had a "Hillary problem"?

The wife of President John Adams
(the second president of the United States)
had so much influence on her
husband during his term in office
from 1797 to 1801 that many
people referred to her as
"Mrs. President."

JEFFERSON'S LEGACY

Whether lusting inside one's heart or lusting inside the White House, it didn't begin with Jimmy Carter. In fact, Thomas Jefferson—the man who is called our greatest president by many—was also the first to face charges of sexual misconduct.

P.S. Many historians now agree that Jefferson was the father of several illegitimate children.

IT'S THE STRANGE CASE OF THOMAS JEFFERSON

Was he a devoted and faithful husband?
Or the kind of guy who likes to mess around
with married women and young girls?

THE THOMAS JEFFERSON STORY, PART ONE

In the beginning there was Betsey Walker. She was pretty and vivacious, and she was also married to Thomas Jefferson's good friend, William George Walker.

Jefferson was such a good friend of the bride and groom the couple asked him to be a member of their wedding party. Not only that, but Thomas Jefferson was such a trusted confidant and buddy to William George that when it was time for him to name an executor of his will, Jefferson was William George's choice.

But then things went awry—terribly awry. On the eve of leaving town for four months to help negotiate a treaty with the Indians at Fort Stanwix, William George took his good friend and neighbor and the executor of his will aside and asked him to keep an eye on his wife while he was gone. Little did he know that Jefferson actually had the hots for his wife and would strike while the cat was away, so to speak.

Only years later as the Walkers were rewriting their wills did William George learn of Jefferson's seduction of his wife; it happened when he told Betsey he intended to keep Jefferson as the executor of his will. She was appalled and told him of the incidents from years ago.

THE THOMAS JEFFERSON STORY, PART TWO

At the age of twenty-eight, Thomas Jefferson married Martha Skelton. Jefferson was a loving and adoring husband, and some say Martha was the love of his life.

The problem is Martha and Thomas were only married for ten years. Then Martha died.

No one has ever suggested that Jefferson cheated on his wife. In fact, when Martha asked him, while on her deathbed, to promise never to marry again, he promised and kept his word for the rest of his life.

THE THOMAS JEFFERSON STORY, PART THREE

For four years Jefferson played the role of the widower—no doubt wearing black for a while, then slowly working his way back into a normal life.

Jefferson was only thirty-nine when Martha died, so we can assume every widow within two hundred miles plied him with casseroles and offers of company and more. He never promised Martha he would abstain from sex, after all.

By 1785, fifteen years before he was elected president, Jefferson was living in Paris and serving as U.S. minister to France.

While attending a party, Jefferson met—and fell in love with—the wife of another man. Her name was Maria Cosway, and by all accounts she was a stunning blonde with a coquettish Italian accent, deep blue eyes, curly locks, and a darling cupid's face.

But let's not be sexist here—the attraction wasn't purely physical. She also charmed the socks off Jefferson intellectually. She was a respected painter. She had a beautiful voice and loved to sing. She was a talented harpsichord player. She was a brilliant conversationalist.As long as Jefferson remained at the party, he found it difficult to leave her side—even though her husband, the renowned Italian painter Richard Cosway, was just on the other side of the room. To prolong the time he could spend in her company, he sent word to the Duchesse de la Rochefoucauld d'Anville, with whom he had dinner plans, that he would need to cancel their previously arranged date.

WEIRD FAMILY VALUES!

Jefferson spent the next eight weeks in the constant company of Maria Cosway. Her husband didn't seem to mind. In fact, he seemed to encourage the affair and often left them alone.

When it was time for the Cosways to return to London, Thomas and Maria made plans to meet in Paris again—this time without Maria's husband in tow. Yet when Maria arrived alone the following August as planned, Jefferson—as we say today—blew her off.

THE THOMAS JEFFERSON STORY, PART FOUR

Over the years there has been much speculation as to why Jefferson would turn a cold shoulder to the woman who sparked such an intense reaction in him the year before. One theory—and our favorite—is that by the time Maria showed up for their next rendezvous he had already taken up with his next paramour.

What woman on earth could replace the beautiful, graceful, and charming Maria Cosway?

One would guess that she might be as young or younger. Probably even more beautiful. And wouldn't you think she'd have to be someone who was more accessible?

Sally Hemings was all of those things and more—she was Jefferson's slave. And she was the half sister of Jefferson's dead wife.

Thomas Jefferson and Sally Hemings were together for thirty-eight years (including Jefferson's eight years as president). Together, they were the parents of more than five children.

THE JEFFERSON ADDENDUM

Let's get this straight: Thomas Jefferson as a forty-eight-year-old man took as his lover a seventeen-year-old girl—who happened to be his slave as well as the half sister of his dead wife?

Sounds impossible, but it's true. Jefferson's wife, Martha Skelton, was the daughter of John Wayles. When John Wayles's third wife died, he took Betty Hemings, a slave, as his concubine, and they had six children, one of whom was Sally. When John Wayles died, he willed the slave children (including Sally) to his daughter Martha and her husband.

• • •

If you want to get technical, Jefferson's idea of a normal life ended when Martha became sick. That's when he resigned from Congress to take care of her. Then, only eight weeks after she died, Jefferson let his friends in government know he was ready to return to the political arena. For that reason, there are those who say that if Martha had lived longer, Jefferson wouldn't have returned to Washington so soon, and he might never have become our third president.

"I've committed adultery in my heart. . . ."

—Jimmy Carter,
in an interview with *Playboy* magazine

"Dan Quayle would rather play golf than have sex any day!"

—Marilyn Quayle

"Mrs. Who?"

When Martin Van Buren wrote his autobiography
after serving as president from 1837 to 1841, he
failed to mention his wife of twelve years.
Not even once.

For what it's worth, Van Buren may not have
even mentioned his father either. Because a
rumor floating around during the mid-1800s
said that President Martin Van Buren was in fact
the illegitimate son of former Vice President
(and traitor and murderer, but we'll
get to that later) Aaron Burr.

DOES SEX SAVE LIVES?

BEN FRANKLIN PROBABLY thought so; he was keeping mistresses well past his seventieth birthday—in an era when the average guy might have considered himself lucky to live to see sixty.

Granted, Ben was never president of the United States, but as one of our Founding Fathers and as a guy who was supposed to be setting an example for his fellow countrymen, his exploits are too good to pass up.

First, there's the story of Ben and Deborah Read. Ben loved Deborah so much that he wanted to marry her. But according to the law he couldn't: A woman who had been married once and then abandoned (as opposed to being divorced or widowed) couldn't get married again.

The punishment for violating this law was pretty stiff: thirty-nine lashes at the public whipping post and a sentence of hard labor for life. So Ben did the next best thing. He asked Deborah to move in and live in sin with him.

Six months later Ben did something even more outrageous: He brought home a son he'd fathered by another woman. On top of that, he also took in his new son's mother so she could be closer to their child. So there were Ben and Deborah and the new baby and the new baby's mom—all living in one house.

Weird family values . . . but they didn't seem to hurt the boy. His name was William Franklin, and he went on to be the governor of New Jersey.

Ben didn't seem to feel any shame about his sexuality either. In fact, he took great pleasure in writing about it. In the essay below, he explains why, given the choice, he always prefers an older mistress over a younger one:

1. Because as they have more Knowledge of the World and their Minds are better stor'd with Observations, their Conversation is more improving and more lastingly agreeable.

2. Because when Women cease to be handsome, they study to be good. To maintain their Influence over Men, they supply the Diminution of Beauty by an Augmentation of Utility. They learn to do 1000 Services small and great and are the most tender and useful of all Friends when you are sick. Thus they continue amiable. And hence there is hardly such a thing to be found as an old Woman who is not a good Woman.

3. Because there is no hazard of Children, which irregularly produc'd may be attended with much Inconvenience.

4. Because thro' more Experience, they are more prudent and discreet in conducting an Intrigue to prevent Suspicion. The commerce with them is therefore safer with regard to your Reputation. And with regard to theirs, if the Affair should happen to be known, considerate People might be rather inclin'd to excuse an old Woman who would kindly take care of a young Man, form his Manners by her good Counsels, and prevent his ruining his Health and Fortune among mercenary Prostitutes.

5. Because in every Animal that walks upright, the Deficiency of the Fluids that fill the Muscles appears first in the highest Part: The Face first grows land and wrinkled; then the Neck, then the Breast, and regarding only what is below the Girdle, it is impossible of two Women to know an old from a young one. And as in the dark all Cats are grey, the Pleasure of corporal Enjoyment with an old Woman is at least equal, and frequently superior, every Knack being by Practice capable of Improvement.

6. Because the Sin is less. The debauching a Virgin may be her Ruin, and make her Life unhappy.

7. Because the Compunction is less. The having made a young Girl miserable may give you frequent bitter Reflections; none of which can attend the making an old Woman happy.

8. [thly and Lastly] They are so grateful! Thus much for my Paradox. But still I advise you to marry directly.

WEIRD FAMILY VALUES!

Meet the hermit of
1600 Pennsylvania Avenue

Her name was Margaret Taylor. She was Zachary Taylor's wife.

All the time she lived at the White House, she hid herself out of sight.

She didn't like all the pomp and circumstance—she said—but this is more likely true:

Ol' Margaret preferred smoking her corncob pipe to talking to the likes of you.

Can you name the president . . .

. . . who once lived with his wife in an apartment so small they had to share a bathroom with the prostitute down the hall?

A. Gerald Ford
B. George W. Bush
C. George H. W. Bush
D. Abraham Lincoln
E. All of the above

(Answer on page 26.)

HERE'S WHAT A FEW OF OUR PAST PRESIDENTS LOOKED FOR IN A WIFE

- When Ulysses S. Grant met Julia Dent, the first thing he noticed was that her eyes were crossed. He fell in love immediately and proposed marriage on the spot.
- Harry Truman met and fell in love with his wife, Bess, when he was six years old. The attraction? She was the only girl in town who could whistle through her teeth.
- While a young senator, JFK once described what he wanted in a wife to a newspaper reporter: "Intelligent, but not too brainy."

AND WHAT ONE FIRST LADY SAW EVEN THOUGH SHE WASN'T LOOKING

IN THE YEARS before she was married, Grace Goodhue was a teacher at an institute for the deaf. While watering the school's garden one day, she looked up and saw a man, wearing only a hat and long underwear, standing in front of a mirror in a nearby boarding house. Surprised by this sight, she let out a laugh.

"He heard me and turned to look at me," Grace later recalled. "When he learned who I was, he managed to arrange a formal introduction—and that is how I became Mrs. Calvin Coolidge."

"Fathers" of Our Country?

1 George Washington is often called "The Father of His Country" even though he never had any children.

2 For what it's worth, James Madison is often called "The Father of the Constitution," but he didn't have any kids either.

3 It's also worth noting that Andrew Jackson raised eleven kids in his lifetime. None of them were his.

BRATS!

- Teddy Roosevelt's son Quentin had his own gang: "The White House Gang." Together, he and his friends did things like drop snowballs off the roof of the White House onto patrolling policemen and throw spitballs at the portraits of earlier presidents.
- Secretary of War Edwin Stanton invented a make-believe military post for his boss Abe Lincoln's son Tad and outfitted the boy with his own Union Army uniform and sword. As a lieutenant, Tad took it upon himself to order additional weapons for the servants, to march the White House guards and other staff members around, and to dismiss guards who weren't performing to his expectations.
- Jesse Grant, Ulysses S. Grant's son, became interested in stamp collecting and ordered some stamps from a mail-order catalog. When the stamps didn't arrive he convinced Kelly, one of the Capitol policemen, to write a letter. "I am a Capitol policeman," Kelly wrote. "I can arrest anybody, anywhere, at any time, for anything. I want you to send those stamps to Jesse Grant. Kelly, Capitol policeman." Jesse's stamps arrived shortly afterward. Jesse also convinced American ambassadors overseas to send him stamps from the countries in which they were stationed. But his interest in stamp collecting waned when his mother made him send thank-you notes to everyone who sent him stamps.
- JFK and Jackie Kennedy hated TV and had all the televisions taken away from the White House when they moved in . . . until Caroline started to cry when it was time for *Lassie* to come on, and they had to have one of the White House servants bring one of the televisions back.

21

OLDER BRATS!

- All three of John Quincy Adams's sons fell in love with the same girl, and she was pretty taken with at least two of them herself. First she got engaged to the middle son, George. Then she married the oldest son, John. George and Charles Francis, the youngest, were pretty steamed at her and refused to attend the wedding. To her credit, the bride did what she could for her two brothers-in-law to make up for her past indiscretions—she named a daughter Georgiana Frances after both of them.

- John Tyler had more kids than any other president—eight by his first wife and seven by his second. He was seventy when the last child, Pearl, was born. He was the first president to get married while in office, but his eight kids from his first wife (who had died) did not approve of the union and refused to attend the wedding.

Perhaps his kids objected to how they met:

John Tyler was entertaining aboard a naval gunship when a cannon exploded and killed three of his guests, including his secretary of state, his secretary of the navy, and New York senator David Gardiner.

Among the remaining guests was Senator Gardiner's young daughter, Julia. When she heard of her father's death, she fainted into the president's arms. He fell in love and four months later the fifty-four-year-old Tyler and the twenty-four-year-old Julia Gardiner were married.

GROVER CLEVELAND'S LOVE-CHILD-OF-THE-MONTH CLUB

GROVER CLEVELAND'S LOVE CHILD #1

FIRST, LET'S DEFINE some terminology: A love child is a child who is conceived out of wedlock. Not such an uncommon thing today, but terribly uncommon in 1884 when Grover Cleveland was running for president.

He was running quite a campaign, too, with a very strong lead over his opponent, until the *Buffalo Evening Telegraph* announced in huge, screaming type that he was the father of an illegitimate son.

So Grover Cleveland did what no sane politician has ever done since, given similar circumstances: He told the truth.

He didn't deny the charges. He didn't try to cover his back. He didn't demand a blood test, and he didn't claim he hadn't inhaled, so to speak.

GROVER'S TRUTH

In 1871, while sheriff of Buffalo, New York, he met a nice woman named Maria Halpin. He liked her. She liked him. Next thing you know, she was in the family way.

It's important to remember that Cleveland was a bachelor when he was dating Maria Halpin—but the same couldn't be said for the other men she was seeing concurrently, any of whom could have been the father.

When Maria came to him with her sad story and demanded that he marry her, he said "No, thank you" but did the next best thing: He offered to provide financial support for the child even though there was a good chance it wasn't his. And he didn't just send money but took an active hand in watching out for the boy's best interests. In fact, at one point when Maria began drinking heavily, Cleveland arranged for her to be institutionalized and for the boy to be adopted by a well-to-do family in New York.

WEIRD FAMILY VALUES!

The more the press (and the public) learned about Grover and the honorable way in which he had handled his relationship with Maria Halpin and the boy, the better he looked.

GROVER CLEVELAND'S LOVE CHILD #2 (SORT OF)

Next thing you know, the newspaper headlines were screaming about another love child. Only this time the love child belonged to Cleveland's opponent, James Blaine.

Turns out Mrs. Blaine gave birth to Junior Blaine only three months after Mr. and Mrs. Blaine were married. That would make Junior love child number two, wouldn't it?

GROVER DOES IT AGAIN

If Grover Cleveland had had his way, no one would ever have known that James Blaine's child was born out of wedlock. In fact, the same informer who leaked the story to the press brought it to Cleveland first. Cleveland read the report, paid the informer, then tore up and burned the evidence. "The other side can have a monopoly on all the dirt," he announced to his shocked and disappointed aides.

Blaine might have learned something from Cleveland about how to deal with the press—but he didn't. Instead of telling the truth, Blaine tried to lie his way out of the story. But lying didn't cut it with the press or the public, and Grover came out ahead at the polls.

GROVER CLEVELAND'S LOVE CHILD #3

The president didn't conceive this love child either—he married her.

Her name was Frances Folsom. She was the daughter of Cleveland's law partner, and she used to call him "Uncle Cleve." Frances was six when her father died and Cleveland became her legal guardian.

Fifteen years later, at the ages of forty-nine and twenty-one respectively, President Grover Cleveland and Frances Folsom were married.

GROVER CLEVELAND'S LOVE CHILD #4

Her name was Ruth. She was the very legitimate daughter of President Cleveland and his wife, Frances.

Unlike the other love children in Grover Cleveland's life, there was nothing scandalous about her—except that Nestle's named a candy bar after her and then kept the White House refrigerator and cabinets well-stocked with food. Ruth's father, the president, whether contractually obligated to do so or not, ended every public appearance he made by saying, "A Ruth in every pot!"

America loved Baby Ruth. Visitors to the White House would find her playing on the lawn and pick her up and pass her around, excited to have had the chance to see her, to touch her.

One day, however, little Ruth stopped going out to play on the lawn. Quickly, rumors spread that she was sick and being hidden from view. A few years later, the rumors proved to be true: Baby Ruth died of cerebral palsy at the age of thirteen.

Answer: George H. W. Bush

2

Sex!

Ever notice there's a big difference between the sex you see in the movies and the sex you have when you get back home? Turns out the same principle applies with presidents.

Movie presidents are usually played by guys like Michael Douglas and Harrison Ford. With a few exceptions, real-life presidents usually have about as much sex appeal as, well, Ronald Reagan. Gerald Ford. Richard Nixon. (Granted, youthful-looking George W. Bush seems to be the exception in this list of Republicans, but looking young isn't necessarily the same thing as being sexy.) Meanwhile, Democratic presidents these days tend to be a little younger, so they also tend to be a little sexier . . . but sexy is kind of relative. After all, with the exception of JFK, we're still talking about guys who look like Bill Clinton and Jimmy Carter.

But presidents get girls, there's no doubt about that.

Occasionally a president or president-to-be will marry and stay faithful to his wife— and, for our purposes, that's the end of that. Other times, they marry one woman and still

A Few Good (Looking) Men

Even Republicans can be good-looking—if you catch them while they're young.

Take Gerald Ford, for example. He appeared on the covers of *Cosmopolitan* and *Look* magazines as a model in the 1930s. And Ronald Reagan won the Most Nearly Perfect Male Figure award from the University of California in 1940.

get others. Or they mess around with women who happen to already be married to someone else.

Sometimes these little indiscretions occur before a president becomes president—but we don't care. Once a president, always a president—even if you're not president yet. Part of acting presidential is to live your life as an open book, allowing the winds of curiosity to blow through all the pages for the world to browse and judge.

Presidential affairs come in a variety of sizes. Some presidents have wee little affairs, so small and insignificant they're barely worth noticing and hardly worth caring about (unless you're the First Lady, of course). Others have bold, brash, obnoxious affairs that involve a troika of ultimate sins—which is to say they have sex with women other than their wives and they do it in such a way so as to ensure that everyone will know about it and they act as if they don't care who (that's you and us and the First Lady and the media) finds out.

PRESIDENTIAL ADULTERY CHART

PRESIDENT: George Washington

CHEATED ON: Martha Custis, his fiancée

CHEATED WITH: Sally Fairfax

THE SCOOP: ### Did George Washington cheat on Martha?

He was tall and broad and handsome. He had a successful career and had inherited a small farm. He was polite and soft-spoken. Yet he courted and wooed a number of women, and none wanted anything to do with him. At one point things got so bad for George Washington in the romance department that after moping around for a while like a lovesick pup, he finally accepted that he would never find a woman to love.

A large part of the problem was that he was already in love. Her name was Sally Fairfax—and she toyed with him and flirted with him and made him feel all light and giddy and gay.

Finally! A woman who would fawn over him and treat him like he was special. Finally! A woman who would respond to his notes of love. Finally! A woman to visit and make love with whenever he could get away from his duties on the front lines of the French and Indian War, where he was commander in chief of the Virginia militia.

Oh, but there were a few minor problems with the relationship: For one thing, Sally was married—to one of George's closest friends, George William Fairfax. And if that wasn't bad enough, the two Georges were practically family because George Washington's half brother Lawrence was married to George William's sister Anne.

In spite of all this, George and Sally carried on for as long as seven years—even after George decided that if he couldn't marry for love, he would at least marry for money, and then got engaged to the richest widow in Virginia, Martha Custis.

Some historians say the relationship between George and Sally never amounted to anything more than a long-term flirtation. Others paint a picture of George riding from battle directly to the home of his love—Sally, not

Martha—on those nights while her husband was away. Most historians agree, however, that once married, George took his duties as a husband very seriously and what physical relationship he had with Sally ended.

Did George Washington cheat on Martha? Obviously that would depend on which version of history you believe and on how you define adultery.

{ My children may be assured that no illegitimate brother or sister exists or ever existed." }

—John Adams

PRESIDENT: **John Adams**

THE SCOOP: **In case you thought sexual liberation and freedom were invented in the sixties, consider this quote from John Adams:**

No father, brother, son, or friend ever had cause of grief or resentment for any intercourse between me and any daughter, sister, mother, or any other relation with the female sex. My children may be assured that no illegitimate brother exists or ever existed.

Implied in this statement, of course, is that while Adams stood by watching, everyone else was doing the wild thing with everyone else—and, given what you are about to read, he was quite right to speak out about his chasteness.

{ For all his prudishness, Adams was not without a sense of humor. In fact, when Adams heard of a rumor that accused him of dispatching General Charles Cotesworth Pickney to England with a U.S. battleship to pick up four pretty girls so he and the general could each keep two as mistresses, Adams replied to a friend: "If this be true, General Pickney has kept them all for himself and cheated me out of my two!" }

PRESIDENT:	Thomas Jefferson

THE SCOOP: In spite of all his sins, he never committed adultery.

PRESIDENTS:	John Quincy Adams, James Madison, James Monroe

THE SCOOP: None for them . . . but there sure were some good rumors going around at the time about Madison's wife, Dolley, and Thomas Jefferson's vice president, Aaron Burr. Of course, by most accounts, these rumors were started by Burr himself.

PRESIDENT:	Andrew Jackson
CHEATED ON:	His wife, Rachel
CHEATED WITH:	His wife, Rachel

THE SCOOP: Every time this president had sex with his wife, he helped her commit adultery again.

Confused? You should be.

Here's what happened: In 1791 Andrew Jackson married Rachel Donelson Robards—or at least he thought he did.

He first met Rachel when he moved into her family's boarding house as a young attorney, and he was taken with her at first sight. Unfortunately for Jackson, Rachel was married. In fact, she was not only married but was married to a man who was given to insane fits of jealous rage.

This was unfortunate for Jackson—who was an honorable guy—because he really liked Rachel and wanted to be her friend.

Unfortunately, Rachel's husband, Captain Lewis Robards, perceived Jackson's overtures of friendship as a threat and flew into such a fit that Rachel had to send word home to her family for help. It was Andrew Jackson who went to her rescue and moved her to the safety of her sister's house in Tennessee.

Through word of mouth Jackson heard that Captain Robards had sought

SEX!

and received a divorce from Rachel in his home state of Kentucky. Very much in love, Jackson quickly approached Rachel's mother and asked for her hand in marriage.

Unfortunately, Jackson was so excited at the prospect of marrying the only woman he had ever loved that he neglected to check the veracity of the second-hand report; in reality Captain Robards's divorce from Rachel was not complete. Therefore, for the first two years of their marriage—until Jackson and Rachel took another marriage vow—Rachel was guilty of adultery with her not-legal husband, Andrew Jackson!

The story gets even more tragic, however. When Jackson ran for president in 1828, incumbent John Quincy Adams and his supporters were relentless in using the story of his "adulterous" marriage to smear Jackson's otherwise popular image. Jackson, who was strong and a fighter, was able to weather the attacks and persevere in his drive to win the presidency. Rachel, on the other hand, did not fare so well. The scandalous charges being made against her honor were more than she could handle—first she slipped into a deep depression. Then, following the election, she had a massive heart attack and died before she even had a chance to see her husband take office.

She was buried three days before Christmas in the gown she had planned to wear to the Inaugural Ball.

PRESIDENT: **Martin Van Buren**

THE SCOOP: **None, although his VP, Richard Johnson, was publicly known to be the father of two illegitimate children. Perhaps Johnson would've married Julia Chinn, his mistress and the mother of his children, if he could have—but the law forbade it as she was black and he was her master.**

PRESIDENTS: **William Henry Harrison, John Tyler, James Polk, Zachary Taylor, Millard Fillmore, Franklin Pierce**

THE SCOOP: **Not a cheater in the bunch.**

PRESIDENT: James Buchanan

CHEATED ON: ???

CHEATED WITH: ???

THE SCOOP: Why did James Buchanan's fiancée commit suicide? [Hint: You can find the answer on page 63.]

    a.   Because she suspected Buchanan had a girlfriend.

    b.   Because she suspected Buchanan had a boyfriend.

    c.   None of the above.

PRESIDENT: Abraham Lincoln

THE SCOOP: He never cheated on his wife. He left her standing at the altar instead.

It's true. It was New Year's Day 1841. Mary Todd was at the appointed place at the appointed time, surrounded by friends, a preacher, and a lot of flowers . . . but Abe never showed. They finally did marry two years later—this time with two hours' notice.

33

PRESIDENT: Andrew Johnson

THE SCOOP: Nope.

PRESIDENT: Rutherford B. Hayes

THE SCOOP: Nothing here.

PRESIDENT: Ulysses S. Grant

THE SCOOP: Nope.

SEX!

PRESIDENT:	James Garfield
CHEATED ON:	Lucretia Garfield
CHEATED WITH:	Lucia Calhoun

THE SCOOP: **The marriage of James and Lucretia Garfield was a rocky one. Once, while a Civil War general all alone in a strange town, he met a woman. He liked her; she liked him. They had an affair.**

Not much is known about Garfield and Mrs. Calhoun because once Mrs. Garfield found out about the affair, she sent her husband back for one last visit with his New York mistress. But he didn't make the trip to make love. Instead, he went back to destroy all the love letters he had sent so they wouldn't surface later and ruin his political career.

PRESIDENT: Chester A. Arthur

THE SCOOP: Nope.

PRESIDENT: Grover Cleveland

THE SCOOP: **See Grover Cleveland's Love-Child-of-the-Month Club on page 23.**

PRESIDENT: William H. Taft

THE SCOOP: Nah.

{ "You can't cast a man as a Romeo who looks and acts so much like an apothecary's clerk." }

—Teddy Roosevelt, of his opponent Woodrow Wilson

WHITE HOUSE: CONFIDENTIAL

PRESIDENT:	Woodrow Wilson
CHEATED ON:	His first wife, Ellen
CHEATED WITH:	Mary Peck

THE SCOOP: *The Many Loves of the Apothecary, Part One*

Wilson and Mrs. Peck met in Bermuda. He needed a rest, his doctor said. But his salary as the president of Princeton University didn't allow him the luxury of taking his wife along.

Mrs. Peck was separated from her wealthy husband and living the high life in Bermuda, hanging out with the governor and Mark Twain and all sorts of other fascinating people.

Wilson's—and Mrs. Peck's—first visit to Bermuda was in 1907. He returned in 1908 and 1910, all the while carrying on an active correspondence with Mrs. Peck in the time in between.

Wilson's relationship with Mrs. Peck made for good newspaper copy when Wilson became a contender for the presidency and when he ran for reelection. When *Mr. Peck* filed for divorce, it was rumored that Wilson was to be named in the suit. It was also rumored that Wilson's letters to Mrs. Peck would be used as evidence. But none of that came to pass.

In reality Wilson had nothing to hide. He had already told his wife about his platonic but treasured friendship with Mrs. Peck, and in an effort to put an end to the rumors once he won the Democratic Party's nomination for the presidency, he took his entire family to Bermuda to meet her.

Later, Mrs. Peck visited the Wilsons at the White House and even spent a day on a shopping spree with Mrs. Wilson.

The Many Loves of the Apothecary, Part Two

While Wilson was president, his wife died of Bright's disease—and it didn't take long for rumors to surface romantically linking Wilson and Mrs. Peck again.

In reality, however, those rumors couldn't have been further from the truth. It was true that Wilson began seeing another woman a year after his wife died and that he did propose to her just two months after they met—but that woman was a widow named Edith Galt, not Mrs. Peck.

Call It a Freudian Slip: After Wilson and Mrs. Galt announced their engagement, the *Washington Post* ran an exclusive front-page story about the couple's first day in public. While the writer of the story reported that the president spent the day "entertaining" his new fiancée, no one at the paper caught the typo that announced in large type:

". . . the President spent the afternoon entering his new fiancée."

PRESIDENT:	Warren G. Harding
CHEATED ON:	His wife, Florence
CHEATED WITH:	Nan Britton and Carrie Phillips
THE SCOOP:	See Mistresses: The Warren G. Harding Way on page 68.

PRESIDENT:	Calvin Coolidge
THE SCOOP:	Old Silent Cal? Nothing to tell.

PRESIDENT:	Herbert Hoover
THE SCOOP:	Are you kidding? Hoover was an engineer.

PRESIDENT: Franklin Delano Roosevelt

CHEATED ON: His wife, Eleanor

CHEATED WITH: Lucy Mercer and Missy LeHand

THE SCOOP: Without presidents like FDR, there wouldn't be books like this one. Or have you already forgotten the stories about FDR and Eleanor that begin on page 3?

PRESIDENT: Harry S Truman

THE SCOOP: Nope.

PRESIDENT: Dwight D. Eisenhower

CHEATED ON: His wife, Mamie

CHEATED WITH: Kay Summersby

THE SCOOP: Ike *almost* had an affair.

While a general during World War Two, Ike had a driver in London who was a very attractive model and actress named Kay Summersby. Later, when he took full command of the European Theatre of Operation, he requested that she be assigned to him as his full-time driver.

According to one account, after the war Eisenhower had written to his superior requesting reassignment in the United States so he could divorce his wife and marry Kay. Kay later wrote a tell-all about her affair with Ike called *Past Forgetting: My Love Affair with Dwight D. Eisenhower.* The irony is, there wasn't much to tell, for according to Summersby, Ike was impotent.

{"This administration's going to do for sex what the last one did for golf."}

—JFK speechwriter Theodore Sorensen

PRESIDENT: John F. Kennedy

CHEATED ON: His wife, Jackie

CHEATED WITH: Perhaps it would be easier to list the names of the few glamorous and beautiful women of the time he didn't sleep with.

THE SCOOP: On second thought, that wouldn't be half as much fun as listing the names of some he allegedly did sleep with: Marilyn Monroe, Jayne Mansfield, Audrey Hepburn, Angie Dickinson, stripper Blaze Starr, and gangster moll Judith Campbell Exner. And let's not forget Marlene Dietrich, who claimed to have slept with JFK and JFK's brother Joe Jr., and JFK's father, Joe Sr. This short list does not include the names of hundreds (yes, hundreds) of other women JFK is said to have slept with. Of course, supplying names of more than a handful of his lovers would be impossible since it is doubtful even Kennedy knew them all by name.

Or, to quote the book *Presidential Sex* by Wesley O. Hagood:

> Jack had numerous sexual encounters with many women. Some were well-known movie stars and burlesque queens. Others were high-class call girls and common prostitutes. His sexual partners also included White House Staffers, secretaries, stewardesses, socialites, campaign workers, and acquaintances of his trusted male friends. Hundreds of others will probably never come to light.

For fun, let's focus on two of his affairs:

Jack Kennedy and Marilyn Monroe: Their regular meeting places included his sister Patricia's home in Santa Monica (she was married to actor Peter Lawford) and the Beverly Hilton Hotel. And they even got together for dalliances at the White House when Jackie was away and when he was aboard *Air Force One.* In 1961 JFK attended a Christmas party at the Lawford home without Jackie and ended up spending several hours alone with Monroe. The entire intimate event, in which the two soaked together in a tub, showered each other with champagne, and more, was caught on tape by a private investigator hired by Jimmy Hoffa, the head of the Teamsters' Union.

The affair led Marilyn to believe the president was going to leave Jackie and marry her . . . which obviously spelled trouble for JFK. Younger brother Bobby was dispatched to delicately make it clear to Marilyn she would never be the First Lady. Once Bobby helped her see the light, he had a passionate affair with her himself. And when she began to have the same delusions about him, he dumped her just as JFK had done.

But Marilyn was stubborn, delusional, and in love. And she had the ear of anyone in the press she wanted—in other words, she represented real danger to the president and the whole of the Kennedy clan. On August 4, 1962, Bobby made a special trip to Los Angeles to convince her their relationship was over. Hours later, she killed herself.

JFK and Judith Campbell Exner: She was Sam Giancana's mistress, and he was a huge mob boss. Of course, when the year is 1960 and you are running for president and you want your friends to introduce you to women who are accessible, willing, and stunningly beautiful, you either need friends in Hollywood (see Jack Kennedy and Marilyn Monroe above) or friends who hang out with gangsters—since gangsters always have beautiful girlfriends hanging around.

Or you could make the process a whole lot easier by having friends who were comfortable in both the world of Hollywood and the world of underground crime.

Those who can read between the lines can see the name Frank Sinatra printed there, for he's the one who introduced the president to Sam Giancana's moll.

What did JFK see in Campbell? Well, she was a stunner, first of all. And second, she had once been Sinatra's mistress, so that added to the appeal. Then, of course, there was the fact that brother Ted had made a pass at her earlier in the evening and had been rebuffed by her—and no Kennedy boy could pass up the chance to best one of his brothers.

The two lovers met all over the country: at the Kennedy home in Georgetown, at a friend's home in Palm Beach, and at the Hilton Hotel in Los Angeles where the Democratic Convention was being held. Once Kennedy was president, the two even met at the White House, and the president once invited Campbell to join him on *Air Force One.*

{ "Yes! I remember her. She was great!" }

—JFK, when aides showed him a snapshot of him and an
unnamed woman sunbathing in the nude

"We Learned It All from Dad!"

In spite of the fact that JFK's father had married into one of the most prominent families in Boston and then fathered nine children (Joe Jr., JFK, Rosemary, Kathleen, Eunice, Patricia, Bobby, Jean, and Teddy), he made a career of womanizing. In the early days of his marriage, he had late-night affairs aplenty with hatcheck girls and women of unsavory reputation. Later, as a Hollywood mogul, his tastes became more refined; he counted among his mistresses stars like Gloria Swanson and a host of others. But you didn't have to be a Hollywood starlet to be one of Joe Sr.'s girls.

Nellie Bly, in her book *The Kennedy Men,* tells this story:

> Jack [JFK] liked to tell friends about the time one of his sisters' friends woke in the middle of the night at Hyannis and saw the Ambassador [JFK's father] standing next to

her bed, beginning to take his robe off as he whispered, "This is going to be something you'll always remember." Jack had watched the scene through a keyhole and took to warning female guests: "Be sure to lock the bedroom door. The Ambassador has a tendency to prowl late at night."

PRESIDENT:	**Lyndon Baines Johnson**
CHEATED ON:	**His wife, Lady Bird Johnson**
CHEATED WITH:	**Alice Glass, Madeline Brown, and many others if you believed LBJ**

THE SCOOP: **LBJ was a known womanizer.**

He earned that reputation because he loved bragging about his exploits. Perhaps the story that best illustrates his attitude toward extramarital affairs occurred while one of his female staffers was with him on a working trip to the Johnson ranch in Texas. In the middle of the night, the staffer reported, a figure in a white sleeping shirt appeared at the foot of her bed. "Move over!" the figure ordered. "This is your president."

Madeline Brown, on the other hand, was more than a one-night stand. She claimed she was LBJ's mistress and sexual plaything for twenty-one years and the mother of his son. In return for satisfying Johnson sexually, LBJ gave Brown a two-bedroom house, a new car every few years, a maid, and the use of a host of credit cards.

41

{"Move over. This is your president."}

—LBJ, to a female staffer after appearing at the foot of her bed in the middle of the night

But when it comes to longevity, Alice Glass had Madeline Brown beat. She met LBJ while he was a young congressman. He was no doubt impressed with Alice's stunning good looks and her intellectual charms; she was impressed with LBJ's commitment to the same causes she was—particularly the wars against poverty, racism, and discrimination. They had an affair that lasted almost thirty years—but after all that time she stopped sleeping with him because she strongly disagreeed with his actions and policies in Vietnam.

$$\left\{ \begin{array}{c} \text{"Of course, I may go into a strange bedroom every} \\ \text{now and then that I don't want you to write about,} \\ \text{but otherwise you can write everything."} \end{array} \right\}$$

—LBJ, in a statement to the press

PRESIDENT:	**Richard Nixon**
CHEATED ON:	**His wife, Pat**
CHEATED WITH:	**Marianna Liu**

THE SCOOP: **Sex and Richard Nixon? Get real!**

Or so we would have thought until we learned about Marianna Liu, a beautiful Chinese cocktail waitress he met in 1958 while on a trip to Hong Kong as Ike's vice president. When Nixon's term as VP ended, he returned again to Hong Kong in 1964, 1965, and 1966 to see Marianna. On one memorable night Nixon and his good friend Bebe Rebozo visited Marianna at The Den, the cocktail lounge where she was hostess. Later that night, Marianna and a friend visited Nixon and Rebozo in their hotel suite to share "drinks and fruit."

Nixon's relationship with Marianna was of special interest to investigators in Hong Kong because Marianna was suspected of being a communist spy. The relationship became of greater interest to them after Nixon declared his candidacy for the presidency. After all, if Nixon became president—and he and Marianna were having an affair and she was a communist spy—any tape recordings and photos or other materials she had could be used to blackmail him and the American government and the American people.

Marianna finally emigrated to the U.S. in 1969, choosing the town of Whittier, California, to settle in. Whittier just happened to be Nixon's hometown. After she became a permanent resident of the United States, she visited Nixon twice at the White House. Their relationship ended shortly afterward, however, because, as one source says, Pat Nixon was "on to it."

PRESIDENT:	**This time, it was the vice president, Nelson Rockefeller**
THE SCOOP:	**Surrounded by good wine and good food and with a beautiful young aide, the vice president was found barefoot and dead. . . .**

Gerald Ford may have kept his nose clean, but his VP, Nelson Rockefeller, died of a heart attack one night at the age of seventy while "editing an art book" with an attractive twenty-five-year-old aide. When paramedics arrived, they found wine and food on the table but no art and no book. Meanwhile, Rockefeller was lying on the floor sans shoes or socks while the aide, Megan Marshak, was dressed in a long black evening gown.

43

{ "I hope you made my grandfather happy." }

—Rockefeller's eighteen-year-old grandson, Steven,
when asked what he would say to Marshak if
he had a chance to meet her

SEX!

PRESIDENT:	Jimmy Carter
CHEATED ON:	His wife, Rosalynn (sort of)
CHEATED WITH:	He didn't really say.

THE SCOOP: While running for president in 1976, Jimmy Carter ended an interview with Playboy magazine with a final thought intended to explain his relationship with God. Instead he put his foot in his mouth:

"I try not to commit a deliberate sin. I recognize that I'm going to do it anyhow because I'm human and I'm tempted. And Christ set some almost impossible standards for us. Christ said, 'I'll tell you that anyone who looks on a woman with lust in his heart has already committed adultery.'

I've looked on a lot of women with lust. I've committed adultery in my heart many times."

PRESIDENT: Ronald Reagan

THE SCOOP: Nothing to tell. (But there were some really good rumors about Nancy and Frank Sinatra.)

PRESIDENT:	George H. W. Bush
CHEATED ON:	His wife, Barbara
CHEATED WITH:	Allegedly with an aide named Jennifer Fitzgerald and others

THE SCOOP: When a CNN reporter asked George H. W. Bush in 1992 about an alleged affair with his longtime aide, Jennifer Fitzgerald, he responded: "I'm not going to take any sleazy questions like that from CNN. I am very disappointed that you would ask such a question of me, and I will not respond to it. I haven't responded in the past, and I think it's an outrage."

It was the first time a reporter had ever asked a sitting president if he had ever had an affair.

Granted, CNN reporter Mary Tillotson displayed bad timing with her question . . . for standing right next to the president at the time was Israel's prime minister, Yitzhak Rabin. However, it is also important to note how Bush answered the question.

Read his response again. He didn't answer.

If you think about it, catching a president at adultery is pretty tricky business. After all, it's all idle speculation unless there's a mistress (or mistresses) who spills her guts or eyewitnesses who spill the beans.

Such is the case of George H. W. Bush—there was a lot of innuendo from Democrats and various members of the press. But it was all circumstantial:

- In the summer of 1992, the cover of *Spy* magazine was devoted to a story called "1,000 Reasons Not to Vote for George Bush." The first reason the article cited for not voting for Bush? *Because he cheats on his wife.*

  The story, by reporter and author Joe Conason, covered the Jennifer Fitzgerald story in detail, and alluded to as many as five other mistresses as well. And even though it was still all circumstantial, Conason summed things up well when he said:

  > If all the proof needed were what people who know him
  > well say in private or off the record about George Bush, he
  > would have been pilloried as a philanderer years ago.

- In 1986 a CNN reporter interviewed Louis Fields, a U.S. ambassador to the Geneva nuclear disarmament talks. Louis confessed that he had once arranged for then Vice President Bush and his aide Jennifer Fitzgerald to "use" a guest house in 1984. "It became very clear to me that the vice president and Ms. Fitzgerald were romantically involved. It made me very uncomfortable." Unfortunately, Fields died in 1988, so he's not available for further comment.

45

- Kitty Kelley, in her biography of Nancy Reagan, tells this story of a group of people having dinner in Washington D.C.:

> "Suddenly, there was a great commotion," recalled one of the five dinner guests, "as the security men accompanying the secretary of state [Alexander Haig] and the attorney general [William French Smith] converged on our table. They started jabbering into their walkie-talkies, and then whispered to Haig and Smith, who both jumped up and left the restaurant. The two men returned about forty-five minutes later, laughing their heads off. They said they had to bail out George Bush, who'd been in a traffic accident with his girlfriend. Bush had not wanted the incident to appear on the D.C. police blotter, so he had his security men contact Haig and Smith. They took care of things for him, and then came back to dinner."

Even though Kelley got this story firsthand from people who were there at the dinner, it's still all just circumstantial evidence.

PRESIDENT:	**Bill Clinton**
CHEATED ON:	**His wife, Hillary Rodham Clinton. And if you want to get literal, you could also say he cheated on the American people.**
CHEATED WITH:	**Gennifer Flowers, Paula Jones, Dolly Kyle Browning, Kathleen Willey (although she claims she was unwilling), Monica Lewinsky, maybe others?**

THE SCOOP: **No need to belabor the point here . . . as the first edition of this book was going to print, we (as in you and us and everyone else in the world) heard the name Monica Lewinsky for the first time.**

At that time, we added a single paragraph about Monica to the book that read:

> As we send this book to press, the Monica Lewinsky story is breaking on the wire. As all of America—and the

world—wonders if he did or didn't, the problem is obvious. When you're a suspected philanderer, you become an easy mark, even if the truth is that you didn't. Stay tuned for details."

Now, eight years later, we think you'll agree that we've all had *enough* details. So we're going to leave it at that.

PRESIDENT:	**George W. Bush**

THE SCOOP: **He was once compelled to tell a reporter at Newsweek: "The answer to the Big A question (adultery) is N-O."**

Laura Bush, however, may have felt at one time that her marriage was at risk because her husband was spending more time with a bottle than with her. As the story goes, she once told him, "It's Jim Beam . . . or me!"

PRESIDENTIAL "SCORE" CARD

WHAT IF PRESIDENTS were ballplayers and it was Katie Couric's job to fill time every night with a lot of meaningless statistics? Suddenly the evening news makes a lot of sense.

A CHRONOLOGICAL CHART OF "SINNERS"*

Years	President(s)	Length of Term	Sinner	Non-Sinner
1789–1797	George Washington	8 years	✔	
1797–1801	John Adams	4 years		✔
1801–1809	Thomas Jefferson	8 years	✔	
1809–1817	James Madison	8 years		✔
1817–1825	James Monroe	8 years		✔
1825–1829	John Quincy Adams	4 years		✔
1829–1837	Andrew Jackson	8 years		✔
1837–1841	Martin Van Buren	4 years		✔
1841–1841	William Henry Harrison	1 month		✔
1841–1845	John Tyler	4 years		✔
1845–1849	James Polk	4 years		✔
1849–1850	Zachary Taylor	16 months		✔
1850–1853	Millard Fillmore	3 years		✔
1853–1857	Franklin Pierce	4 years		✔

* As defined by Jimmy Carter.

Years	President(s)	Length of Term	Sinner	Non-Sinner
1857–1861	James Buchanan	4 years	✔	
1861–1865	Abraham Lincoln	4 years		✔
1865–1869	Andrew Johnson	4 years		✔
1869–1877	Ulysses S. Grant	8 years		✔
1877–1881	Rutherford B. Hayes	4 years		✔
1881–1881	James Garfield	2.5 months	✔	
1881–1885	Chester Alan Arthur	4 years		✔
1885–1889	Grover Cleveland	4 years	✔	
1889–1893	Benjamin Harrison	4 years		✔
1893–1897	Grover Cleveland	4 years	✔	
1897–1901	William McKinley	4 years		✔
1901–1909	Theodore Roosevelt	8 years		✔
1909–1913	William Howard Taft	4 years		✔
1913–1921	Woodrow Wilson	8 years		✔
1921–1923	Warren G. Harding	2 years	✔	
1923–1929	Calvin Coolidge	6 years		✔
1929–1933	Herbert Hoover	4 years		✔
1933–1945	Franklin D. Roosevelt	12 years	✔	
1945–1953	Harry Truman	8 years		✔
1953–1961	Dwight D. Eisenhower	8 years	✔	

SEX!

Years	President(s)	Length of Term	Sinner	Non-Sinner
1961–1963	John F. Kennedy	2 years	✔	
1963–1969	Lyndon B. Johnson	6 years	✔	
1969–1974	Richard Nixon	5 years	✔	
1974–1977	Gerald Ford	3 years		✔
1977–1981	Jimmy Carter	4 years	✔*	
1981–1989	Ronald Reagan	8 years		✔
1989–1993	George H. W. Bush	4 years	✔	
1993–2001	Bill Clinton	8 years	✔	
2001–	George W. Bush			✔

By his definition, not ours.

D-I-Y SIN CHART:
HOW TO CALCULATE WHICH PARTY
HAS HAD MORE "SINNERS"* IN THE WHITE HOUSE

- There have been forty-two presidents including George W. Bush.
- Although Grover Cleveland served two nonconsecutive terms as our twenty-second and twenty-fourth president, he only counts once in the head count above.
- It wasn't until the election of 1852, when Franklin Pierce was elected, that the two-party system as we know it came into existence. For that reason the following statistics apply only to the years 1852 to 2006. The one exception was the election of Andrew Johnson to vice president in 1864; he was a Democrat nominated for VP by the Republicans and elected with Lincoln on the National Union ticket.
- Since the election of 1852, twenty-nine men have served as president—eleven as Democrats and eighteen as Republicans.
- Since the election of 1852, a Republican president has been in the White House for eighty-six years and a Democrat for sixty-eight years.

* *As defined by Jimmy Carter.*

51

"SINNERS"* BY PARTY

Democrats	Republicans	Third Party
1. James Buchanan	1. James Garfield	1. George Washington (Federalist)
2. Grover Cleveland	2. Warren G. Harding	2. Thomas Jefferson (Democrat-Republican)
3. Franklin D. Roosevelt	3. Dwight D. Eisenhower	
4. John F. Kennedy	4. Richard Nixon	
5. Lyndon B. Johnson	5. George Bush	
6. Jimmy Carter**		
7. Bill Clinton***		

* As defined by Jimmy Carter.
** Again, by his definition, not ours.
*** The attempted cover-up of an extra-marital affair at the White House led to his impeachment.

PRESIDENTIAL MISTRESS*/ GIRLFRIEND** NAMING CHART

JUST A LITTLE advice for parents: If you want to give your daughter the best odds of growing up to be the mistress or girlfriend of the president, just give her a name that is some variation of Mary. Second runner-up: Jennifer (if you want your daughter to grow to have an affair with a Republican) or Gennifer (if you want to see her playing around with a Democrat).

President	Alleged Mistress	Alleged Girlfriend	Other
George Washington	Sally Fairfax (married)		
Thomas Jefferson		Betsey Walker (married)	
		MARIA Cosway (married)	
		Sally Hemings (underage slave)	
James Buchanan			William D. King
James Garfield	Mrs. Calhoun		
Grover Cleveland		**MARIA** Halpin (may have conceived an illegitimate child together)	
Warren G. Harding	Nan Britton		
		Carrie Philips	
FDR	Lucy Mercer		
	MARguerite (Missy) LeHand		
Dwight D. Eisenhower	Kay Summersby		

*A presidential mistress is defined as a woman who has been involved with a married president.
**A presidential girlfriend is defined as a woman who has been involved with a bachelor president under immoral circumstances.

SEX!

President	Alleged Mistress	Alleged Girlfriend	Other
John F. Kennedy	**MAR**ilyn Monroe		
	MARlene Dietrich		
	Jayne Mansfield		
	Angie Dickinson		
	Blaze Starr		
	Judith Campbell Exner, etc.		
LBJ	Alice Glass		
	Madeline Brown		
Richard Nixon	**MAR**Ianna Liu		
George H. W. Bush	**JENNIFER** Fitzgerald		
Bill Clinton	**GENNIFER** Flowers		

3

Scandal!

D UH!"

That's the sound of a really good presidential scandal once it makes the news and reaches your average guy or gal on the street. It's usually followed up with "How could this guy, the president, be so stupid?" or "How could he be so stupid that he actually got caught?"

The measure of a good scandal is the look on the president's face at the moment he gets nailed. Then comes the denial, the st-st-stuttering attempt to explain, or the dance to place blame on the back of someone else. And that's when the show starts to get good.

Let's define a good scandal, shall we? Essentially, there are two types:

1. The first begins with an event or set of circumstances that is not very important yet is easily described in a few words or sentences and is easily blown out of proportion by the press. From a consumer's point of view, this type of scandal is one that leaves

us all with an insatiable desire to know more. And every time another fact or angle is added to the story, it sounds even more ludicrous or surreal or dumb than it did before, driving us to want to know even *more*.

2. The second type of scandal is more serious. It usually involves a serious breach of security or confidence or trust, yet is equally as dumb.

Bill Clinton's two-hundred-dollar haircut on a runway at LAX was a good scandal of the former variety. Ronald Reagan's Iran-Contra affair is a fine example of the latter.

ALEXANDER HAMILTON'S BLACKMAILING MISTRESS

IT JUST GOES to show you that you don't have to be president to create a presidential-sized scandal.

Just ask Alexander Hamilton, a guy who was secretary of the treasury and might have become president one day if Vice President Aaron Burr hadn't killed him first.

When it came to politics, Hamilton may have been smart. But as the following story shows, when it came to having an affair, he was a real sucker.

IN A NUTSHELL, HAMILTON WAS SET UP

It was a beautiful plan, one created by a sultry and seductive woman named Maria Reynolds (yet another of our fearless leaders finds himself compromising his virtue with yet another woman named Maria) and her husband, James, who was a con man. It worked like this:

- First, Maria paid a visit to Hamilton at his office and told him a long and tragic tale of being deserted by her husband (which was a lie).

- Next, she lured him back to her house for a tryst—for which Hamilton paid her handsomely. The payment, no doubt, was Hamilton's way of helping Maria deal with the financial aspect of her desertion plight.
- Now the plot thickened . . . for in walked Maria's husband.

HAMILTON HAS A PROBLEM

From a blackmailer's perspective, it doesn't get any better than this—Hamilton had a wife, a reputation, and a future in politics to protect. And here is where James and Maria Reynolds proved they were not your common low-life blackmailers wanting to make a quick buck and run. No, what they had in mind for Hamilton was a long-term financial plan.

James Reynolds's initial reaction to finding his wife with another man was one of shock and horror—his wife was taken from him! His home was broken! His heart would never heal! (Of course, Reynolds was only acting; this was all part of a larger plan.)

On second thought, James Reynolds said to Alexander Hamilton, maybe this isn't such a bad thing after all. You seem to like Maria, she seems to like you, and she seems to be in a better mood after she has seen you. If you'll just pay me a thousand dollars, you can sleep with my wife any time you like, and no one has to be any wiser.

The attraction was mutual—James and Maria liked Hamilton's money, and Hamilton was infatuated with Maria. The affair continued for almost a year.

After Hamilton paid him the first thousand dollars James Reynolds of course continued to ask for more. Hamilton paid it, at times even borrowing money from friends to keep James and Maria happy.

The World According to James Reynolds:

"You took advantage of a poor Broken harted woman. . . . You have acted the part of the most Cruelest man in existence. . . . Now Sire you have bin the Cause of Cooling [of] her affections for me."

—James Reynolds, before Hamilton paid him off

"I find when ever you have been with her, she is Cheerful and kind, but when you have not in some time she is Quite the Reverse."

—Reynolds, after Hamilton paid him off

AND BABY MAKES FOUR

This cash-for-sex relationship with James and Maria Reynolds continued for almost a year until Maria got pregnant and threatened to kill herself. To Hamilton, this looked like a smart time to bow out. However, James Reynolds saw things differently: He decided it was the perfect time to ask for more than money—this time he tried to blackmail Hamilton into giving him a nice, cushy government job.

This is where Hamilton drew the line. His personal life was his own to make a mess of, he reasoned, but to his credit, he was completely unwilling to compromise his position or the public trust.

James, on the other hand, figured that if he couldn't get a government appointment or any more money out of Hamilton, then he could certainly earn some cash by taking the entire story to Hamilton's political enemies in Congress.

HAMILTON SPILLS HIS GUTS

On December 15, 1792, Democrat Alexander Hamilton responded to a knock at his door and opened it to discover three Republican congressmen—James Monroe, Frederick Muhlenburg, and Abraham Venable—standing on his doorstep and ready to string him up.

James Reynolds, it seems, not only told these three congressmen about Hamilton's affair, but he also led them to believe Hamilton had used government funds to pay him off.

As Hamilton saw it, if he was going to avoid hanging right there or public humiliation later, he had to convince the three guys in his living room that, while on a personal level his actions were immoral, he hadn't done anything to compromise his position as secretary of the treasury. And the only way Hamilton could see to convince these guys, his political enemies, was to tell them every last detail of the affair and to document his story with a well-laid paper trail. Hamilton's story was so convincing and so well-documented—he had signed receipts for money borrowed from friends, signed receipts he had given to James, and love letters he had received from Maria—that the three congressmen could in no way doubt his story.

SCANDAL!

The three congressmen heard him out. As much as they would have liked to use the story to destroy him, they were concerned that a scandal of this nature, involving such a high-ranking member of the government when the Union was so young, could destroy the people's confidence in their leaders and their nation—and so all three agreed to carry Hamilton's story to the grave.

Hamilton's story remained secret for six years until a written transcript of his confession was leaked to the press and published. Hamilton quickly retaliated with his own published response that, interestingly, went on to become a huge bestseller.

The Reynolds Wrap-Up

Here's how the saga of James and Maria Reynolds ended:

- Maria eventually divorced James and married another con man.
- Maria's attorney for her divorce was none other than Aaron Burr.
- Maria was not only an adulteress; she was also a bigamist. It seems she got married again thirty minutes before Burr got her divorce finalized.

EVERYTHING WE KNOW ABOUT [BAD] KARMA
WE LEARNED FROM VICE PRESIDENT AARON BURR:

- He was the first presidential candidate to lose the presidency by a vote of the House of Representatives.
- Next, he was passed over by his own party for reelection as vice president.
- Finally, that lug Alexander Hamilton called him "despicable" and "dangerous" and, well, what else could Burr do but challenge him to a duel and kill him?
- But what goes around comes around: Aaron Burr died in 1836 at the age of eighty a forgotten man without a cent to his name in a hotel on Staten Island in New York City.

61

SCANDAL!

Was James Buchanan
America's first gay president?

—

Was William Rufus DeVane King
America's first gay vice president?

—

Were the president and the
vice president having an affair?

Confused? Read on. . . .

WAS HE OR WASN'T HE?

THIS IS A story of sexual intrigue that involves a president, a vice president, a fiancée, and a closet.

Although they were president and vice president during different administrations, James Buchanan and William Rufus De Vane King may have been the first gay men to occupy the executive offices of the United States of America. They met as members of Congress. King was elected to the Senate from the state of Alabama at the age of thirty-three in 1819. Buchanan was elected to the Senate from the state of Pennsylvania at the age of forty-three in 1834.

From the moment they met, they were inseparable. For years, they were known as "Miss Nancy and Aunt Fancy" or "Mr. Buchanan and his wife" and King was often referred to as "Mrs. B." or "Buchanan's better half."

DID BUCHANAN'S FIANCÉE KILL HERSELF WHEN HE TOLD HER THE NEWS?

At the age of twenty-eight, Buchanan was engaged to Anne Coleman, who died suddenly of mysterious causes. The truth of her death remains unknown, but many historians believe she committed suicide.

This much is known: Buchanan never became romantically involved with another woman for the rest of his life.

OR . . . WAS JAMES BUCHANAN "OUTED"?

A day after Anne's death, Buchanan sent a letter to her father:

My Dear Sir:

You have lost a child, a dear, dear child. I have lost the only earthly object of my affections, without whom life now presents to me a dreary blank. My prospects are all cut off, and I feel that my happiness will be buried with her in the grave. It is now no time for explanation, but the time will come when you will discover that she, as well as I, have been much abused. God forgive the authors of it. My feelings of resentment against them, whoever they may be, are buried in the dust. I have now one request to make, and, for the love of God and of your dear departed daughter whom I loved infinitely more than any other human being could love, deny me not. Afford me the melancholy pleasure of seeing her body before its internment. I would not for the world be denied this request.

I might make another, but from the misrepresentations which must have been made to you, I am almost afraid. I would like to follow her remains to the grave as a mourner. I would like to convince the world, and I hope yet to convince you, that she was infinitely dearer to me than life. I may sustain the shock of her death, but I feel that happiness has fled from me forever. The prayer which I make to God without ceasing is, that I yet may be able to show my veneration for the memory of my dear departed saint, by my respect and attachment for her surviving friends.

May Heaven bless you, and enable you to bear the shock with the fortitude of a Christian. I am, forever, your sincere and grateful friend,

James Buchanan

Anne Coleman's father returned the letter unopened.

WILL THE "REAL" STORY BEHIND ANNE COLEMAN'S DEATH EVER BE KNOWN?

At one point in his seventies, James Buchanan seemed ready to reveal the details of his relationship with her and the cause of her death. He told a friend he had deposited documents at a bank in New York that would explain his relationship with Miss Coleman.

Unfortunately, after Buchanan died his executors found a handwritten note with the documents instructing them to destroy the papers without reading them . . . and they followed his instructions to the letter.

SCANDAL!

THE STRANGE CASE OF THE ALCOHOLIC AND THE DYING MAN

A FURTHER SCANDAL INVOLVING WILLIAM RUFUS DEVANE KING

WHILE RUNNING AS Franklin Pierce's vice-presidential candidate, King didn't do a single day of campaigning.

Why? Because he was holed up in Havana dying of tuberculosis.

President-to-be Franklin Pierce wasn't in much better shape: He was such a heavy drinker that Republicans would taunt him by calling him "a hero . . . of many a well-fought bottle."

While Pierce was able to control his drinking well enough to make it through four years in the White House, King didn't have the same luck. He was so sick that he didn't even make it back to Washington for his own inauguration. Instead, by a special act of Congress, he was allowed to be sworn into office in Cuba—in fact, he's the only executive officer of the United States who has ever been sworn in on foreign soil. King died six weeks after taking office and didn't spend a single day of his vice-presidential term in the capital city.

WARREN G. HARDING GETS EXISTENTIAL

Duh-mb!

When it became apparent that the charming, handsome Ohio newspaperman Warren Harding was to be a strong contender for the Republican presidential nomination in 1920, a group of party heavies whisked him into a "smoke-filled" hotel room to grill him about his past and any skeletons he might have to hide. When asked directly, Harding responded by dismissing himself from the room for a break. He was gone for close to ten minutes, and when he returned he told the waiting Republicans there wasn't anything he was hiding that would surface later and harm his reputation.

Perhaps Harding misunderstood the question. While the party bosses wanted to know if he had any skeletons to hide, Harding must have thought they just wanted to make sure all his skeletons were well hidden.

"Where'd you go, Warren G. Harding?"

Of course, you might choose to believe he was so excited at the prospect of being nominated president that he had to make a quick trip to the bathroom. Most historians, however, figure he slipped out to make a few phone calls. To his mistress. Or mistresses. To beg for their silence.

It worked too. Until Harding dropped dead.

MISTRESSES: THE WARREN G. HARDING WAY

HOW TO FIND 'EM

Option #1: If you've got friends and they've got wives, why bother looking anywhere else?   Carrie Phillips was the wife of Harding's good friend Jim Phillips. The Harding-Phillips affair lasted for fifteen years.

Option #2: Let her come to you.   Harding and Nan Britton first met when she was a young teen. He owned the *Marion Star* newspaper, and she had a secret schoolgirl crush on him and wrote short bits of news for his paper about the activities and students at her school.

Seven years later, when she was twenty-one and living in New York and he was a fifty-one-year-old senator, she contacted him and asked if he could help her get a job.

He could and he did. He took her to a hotel, rented the bridal suite, and offered her a job as his mistress.

Ironically, Nan Britton was a virgin at the time—but that didn't last long. Soon she and the senator were meeting at various hotels and eventually in his Senate offices. After he was elected president, they met regularly in a White House closet (which was later made famous by Bill Clinton and Monica Lewinsky) and in the homes of various Harding friends.

"Whatcha got to hide, Warren G. Harding?"

Plenty!

- A mistress named Carrie Phillips
- Another mistress named Nan Britton
- An illegitimate daughter named Elizabeth Ann Britton

HOW TO HIDE 'EM

Option #1: Send her away . . . for life, if you can.   Imagine you're the head of the Republican National Committee and you discover your presidential candidate lied to you about his mistresses in that smoke-filled room. Quick! What do you do? How do you keep the press (and the American public) from finding out?

One way: Try to send them away to a place where the press will never find them. And send them away for life, if you can.

Believe it or not, this worked with Carrie Phillips. When Harding's campaign manager offered her $25,000 on the spot and $2,000 a month (in 1920 dollars!) to take a long vacation until Harding left office, she took him up on the deal and stayed away until after Harding died.

SCANDAL!

Option #2: Tell her you love her.   Given the amount of attention that Harding heaped upon Nan, there was no way she was going to ruin a good thing by squealing to the press.

Harding sent Nan hundreds of explicit love letters, letters that ran as long as forty pages in length. Ironically, given Harding's background as a newspaperman, he often chose a pencil and little pieces of scrap paper on which to pour out his deep feelings of love and passion.

WHATEVER HAPPENED TO NAN BRITTON?

The one good thing you could say about Harding was that he really knew how to make friends and how to keep them. The fact that he could get both of his mistresses (and a host of others) to remain quiet about his clandestine affairs during the two and a half years of his presidency was nothing short of a miracle.

Once he died, however, all bets were off. Take the case of Nan Britton. Of course Harding supplied her with money. Of course he told her he loved her. Of course he led her to believe that he would marry her when his wife died. But he ended up dying before his wife did, and no money was set aside for Nan or their daughter. So Nan took matters into her own hands.

First, she tried contacting Harding's family for child support, but they shooed her away. So she naturally did what all good Americans do when in similar straits: She wrote a book. It was called *The President's Daughter,* and it was published by the Elizabeth Ann Guild. Elizabeth Ann, of course, was the name of Nan's daughter by Harding, and Britton claimed she would use

An Illegitimate Father?

Although Elizabeth Ann looked a lot like him, Harding had absolutely no desire to see her. In fact, Nan Britton reported in her book that she could barely get Harding to even look at a photo of her.

Elizabeth Ann was Harding's only child.

the money from the sale of the book to help other unwed mothers and illegitimate children.

She must have been able to give others a lot more help than Harding ever gave to her—the book was a runaway bestseller and was made into the movie *Children of No Importance* in 1928.

POSTSCRIPT TO THE WARREN HARDING STORY

AMONG HISTORIANS, IT is almost universally accepted that Harding was one of the worst presidents in history.

From the moment he lied about his past in that hotel room, the tone was set for a presidency beset with more lies, corruption, favoritism, and general ineptitude.

The truth about the corruption and favoritism of his administration began to seep out while he was still in office. Financial scandals were uncovered, and members of his cabinet resigned and even committed suicide. But the real truth about Harding's presidency wasn't exposed until after he died.

THE PEGGY EATON AFFAIR

NEITHER OF YOUR authors has ever been president, nor do they ever intend to be. But they do have one piece of wisdom to share with you should you ever wind up with the job: Don't ever let your domestic or foreign policy be determined by friends and their domestic problems, as President Andrew Jackson once did.

It all started with President Jackson's friend Senator John Eaton of Tennessee. Senator Eaton had a friend named Peggy Timberlake. Peggy Timberlake had a husband named Captain Timberlake.

Since Captain Timberlake spent a lot of time at sea, Peggy would often get lonely. In fact, she was what they used to call "a woman of ill repute." The truth is she had a bad reputation with townfolks before Senator Eaton came around—and hanging out with the likes of him didn't help.

One day, Captain Timberlake washed up dead. And President Jackson, with the scandalous affair and death of his own wife, Rachel (see page 31), very much on his mind, urged his friend Senator Eaton to make an honest woman of the now-widowed Mrs. Timberlake. The senator took the president's advice.

So far, so good.

Now, in a totally unrelated move, President Jackson appointed Senator Eaton to the position of secretary of war. While there was no real dispute about Eaton's qualifications to serve in the position, all the society ladies of Washington were appalled. Why? Because if Senator Eaton became secretary of war, it would mean a woman with the former Mrs. Timberlake's virtues, as a result of her new husband's appointment, would necessarily have to be allowed to become a member of the Washington wives' inner circle of friends.

Jackson, meanwhile, discounted all the rumors about the new Mrs. Eaton's past and discounted the talk of a Washington Wives revolt. Instead he ordered all members of his administration to order all their wives to treat the new Mrs. Eaton with all the dignity and respect her position deserved.

One woman who refused to abide by the president's order was the wife of his own vice president, John Calhoun. President Jackson was so frustrated by Mrs. Calhoun that he called on her at home himself with the intention of delivering the order to her face. However, the will of President Jackson was no match for the will of Floride Calhoun. Not only did she ignore the president's order to treat Mrs. Eaton with respect, but she gave an order of her own: She told her butler to show the president to the door.

Was Jackson's Reasoning Sound?

When Eaton confided in Jackson about Peggy Timberlake's checkered past, the president pointed out that "your marrying her will disprove these charges, and restore Peggy's good name."

It never occurred to President Jackson that his entire cabinet could come unraveled over a scandal involving so small a domestic issue as the reputation of one appointed member's wife. But it did. Given the circumstances that led to the undoing of his own beloved wife's reputation and her death from a heart attack shortly afterward, this entire episode was particularly troubling to President Jackson.

Determined to put things in order and set matters right, President Jackson held a formal dinner for all of his cabinet members and arranged for Peggy Eaton to sit in the seat of honor beside him. The move was intended to send a message to the wives of the other cabinet members. Meanwhile, Mrs. Eaton's choice of attire for the evening didn't do much to help the president's cause; she wore a low-cut dress that covered only one shoulder, which only served to feed the flames of controversy.

President Jackson refused to call a single meeting of his cabinet as long as their wives refused to treat Mrs. Eaton as one of their equals. Therefore, instead of cabinet meetings Jackson held what his enemies called "Kitchen Cabinet" meetings—meetings with trusted friends and advisers who did not hold high public offices but were highly valued

Jackson may have been the first to have an informal cabinet but he wasn't the last:

Teddy Roosevelt had a *Tennis Cabinet,* Warren Harding had a *Poker Cabinet,* and Herbert Hoover had a *Medicine Ball Cabinet* because he liked to toss one of the heavy balls around while he talked.

and trusted by President Jackson. They were called the Kitchen Cabinet because they usually met in the White House kitchen and snuck in and out through the back door, passing relatively unnoticed.

PEGGY EATON, PRESIDENT-MAKER?

The guy who benefited the most from the Eaton affair was President Jackson's secretary of state, Martin Van Buren. He was one of the few members of Jackson's administration who could afford to be polite and courteous and attentive toward Mrs. Eaton without risking reprisals at home from his own wife. He was, after all, a widower.

It was Van Buren, in fact, who finally solved the "Petticoat War," as it was called, since the women of Washington were unwilling to let their cause die. His solution was that the president should replace the entire cabinet, letting the pro-Eaton members (like Van Buren and Eaton himself) resign before dismissing the remaining anti-Eaton members. Once he was free of the other members, the president could choose a new Peggy Eaton-friendly cabinet and give his friends Eaton and Van Buren new appointments that were sure to please.

Jackson repaid Van Buren for his brilliant political solution by guaranteeing him his nomination for vice president in the next election.

4

Impeachment!

Uh-oh. It's the "I" word.

No doubt it's a word that presidents would rather not think about, which is a fine thing since impeachment mostly hasn't been a big part of the story when it comes to the history of American presidents.

But we also must point out that this does seem to be changing, as over the past few years it's become more and more common to hear talk about impeaching the president—whomever the current president may be.

18½-MINUTE GAP ENDS 106-YEAR GAP

A BRIEF HISTORY OF IMPEACHMENT IN SIX QUICK SENTENCES

1. In 1776, as a reaction to being royally screwed by British royalty for a few hundred years, American colonists added "impeachment clauses" to their colonial constitutions to ensure that they could give government officials the boot if they were doing a rotten job or if they were taking advantage of their positions.

2. In 1787, about five minutes after the framers of the U.S. Constitution decided that they would have a government led by a president, they laid down the law as to how they could *remove* this president from office if they ever needed to.

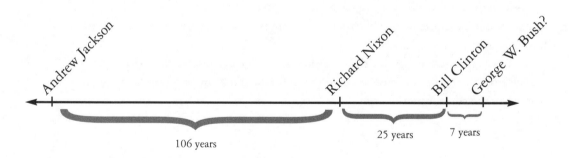

By the way, we're not supporting or advocating a Bush impeachment; we're merely making the point that as of the time of this writing, it is being publicly discussed.

3. In 1868, the House of Representatives passed articles of impeachment against President Andrew Johnson for what, in retrospect, were reasons that were mostly politically motivated.
4. 106 years later, in 1974, the House of Representatives passed articles of impeachment against President Richard Nixon for misconduct related to the Watergate cover-up.
5. 25 years later, in 1999, President Bill Clinton was impeached.
6. 7 years later, in 2006, talk swirls of yet another impeachment.

Newsflash!

Just to prove our point about how common talk of impeachment has become, as we write this, the headline of a current story at WashingtonPost.com reads:

Democrats Are Split As Impeachment Whispers Get Louder

—WashingtonPost.com,
March 25, 2006

13 OTHER IMPEACHMENTS THAT GOT AWAY

CONSIDER THE PROCESS by which an impeachment begins. Logically, it must start with one loud disgruntled voice, followed by a growing chorus of agreement from others.

Everyone knows Andrew Johnson and Bill Clinton were impeached yet never convicted. But have you ever wondered how many other presidents have faced a growing chorus calling for their impeachment but somehow managed to kill the impeachment movement before it could make it to the House and Senate for a vote?

To answer that question, we use personal anecdotes, regional newspaper coverage, and of course stories from the *New York Times* to compile this list of impeachment near-misses.

President: Abraham Lincoln

Year: Around 1862

They said: According to the memoirs of Pennsylvania Senator and Secretary of War, Simon Cameron: "while I was resting at my home in Pennsylvania, that I received from a number of most prominent gentlemen an invitation to visit Washington and attend a consultation which was to be held in regard to national affairs . . . I went to the capital and found assembled there a number of most influential gentlemen, who had come together ostensibly for the purpose of advising together regarding the condition of the country. This, I say, was their ostensible purpose for calling the meeting, but I soon found that their real object was to find means by which the President could be impeached and turned out of office."

The issue: Slavery? Nope. According to Cameron, "The complaint against Mr. Lincoln was that he lacked ability and energy, and that he was not pushing the war with sufficient vigor."

President: Rutherford B. Hayes

Year: 1878

They said: According to the *Raleigh* (North Carolina) *Observer:*
             "If the truth implicates Mr. Hayes, let him be impeached"

The issue: It was called "The Compromise of 1877." Hayes received fewer popular votes than his opponent, Samuel Tilden, but neither candidate had the 185 required Electoral College votes to declare victory. In fact, the election was a real cliffhanger, because Hayes had 165 electoral votes and Tilden had 184, which meant that Tilden only needed *one more* electoral vote to win. Meanwhile, there were exactly 20 votes unaccounted for, and Hayes would need all 20 to win. *So how did Hayes emerge the winner?* Largely through a back-room bargain called the "Compromise of 1877," in which Rutherford representatives quietly promised Southern Democrats that Rutherford would pull federal troops from the South in exchange for their support. Because of the highly disputed way Rutherford won the election, he was often called "Rutherfraud" and "His Fraudulency." And, of course, the results of the hotly contested election also led to talk of impeachment.

President: William Howard Taft

Year: 1912

They said   According to Washington Senator Miles Poindexter: "It is flagrant enough in my judgment to justify impeachment."

The issue: Poindexter objected to President Taft removing from office various supporters of Theodore Roosevelt.

President: Woodrow Wilson

Year: 1919

They said: Headline from the September 11, 1919, *New York Times:* CHICAGO CHEERS SENATE RADICALS, ATTACKS MADE ON WILSON
Cries of "Impeach Him!" Punctuate Borah's Plea Not to Give President More Power

The issue: The problem was Woodrow Wilson's "League of Nations," which would require the United States to make its troops available to defend other nations.

President: Herbert Hoover

Year: 1932

They said: From the December 14, 1932, *New York Times:* DEBT BETRAYAL CHARGED: Chamber Is Amazed by Pennsylvania Republican's Sudden Attack on the President

The issue: The charge was that Hoover was harming United States interests by forgiving foreign debt.

IMPEACHMENT!

President: Franklin Delano Roosevelt

Year: 1935

They said: To quote Republican Congressman Hamilton Fish of New York: "The President has usurped the powers of Congress and it is time we called a halt."

The issue: Republicans condemned Roosevelt for not balancing the budget and believed his aggressive New Deal economic reforms should be left up to the states to implement and run.

President: Franklin Delano Roosevelt

Year: 1941

They said: Headlines from the March 3, 1941, *New York Times:* NYE 'NO WAR' PLEA CHEERED: DETROIT CROWD SHOUTS 'IMPEACH THE PRESIDENT'

The issue: In March 1941, Roosevelt signed the "Lend-Lease Act" which gave him the power to lend arms and other war materials to other nations if it was in the country's best interest to do so. The president signed the act as a way to be able to support ally Great Britain in World War II without formally declaring war on Italy or Germany.

President: Harry Truman

Year: 1950

They said: To quote Senator Joseph McCarthy, Republican of Wisconsin: "[T]he time is long overdue for the congress, in the name of America, to stand up and be counted and immediately impeach you, Mr. President."

The issue: McCarthy objected to Truman's refusal to accept aid from Chiang Kaishek's Chinese Nationalist troops in Korea.

President: Harry Truman

Year: 1951

They said: To quote Senator William E. Jenner, Republican of Indiana: "I charge that this country today is in the hands of a secret coterie which is directed by agents of the Soviet Union. We must cut this whole cancerous conspiracy out of our Government at once. . . . Our only choice is to impeach President Truman and find out who is the secret invisible government which has so cleverly led our country down the road to destruction."

The issue: Truman relieves General Douglas Macarthur from his command of U.S. and UN forces in Korea.

President: Harry Truman
Year: 1951
They said: Truman, to Republican Senator Charles W. Tobey of New Hampshire: "Now let me tell you this, Senator. If you want to have me impeached, you just go right ahead and I'll help you."
The issue: Truman told Tobey that he had "good information" that "a great many" members of Congress were getting kickbacks for helping members of the public acquire loans through the government's Reconstruction Finance corporation. Tobey believed that that the president's accusation about members of Congress was an impeachable offense.

President: Harry Truman
Year: 1952
They said: Headline from the June 5, 1952, *New York Times:* MOVES TO IMPEACH TRUMAN POSTPONED
The issue: To prevent a shutdown of American steel mills, Truman had them seized by the federal government.

President: Lyndon Johnson
Year: 1968
They said: Headline from the January 18, 1968, *New York Times:* NEW GROUP SEEKING TO IMPEACH JOHNSON
The issue: A group called Citizens for Governmental Restraint claimed that LBJ violated the Constitution by sending American troops to Vietnam.

President: Ronald Reagan
Year: 1983
They said: Headline from the November 11, 1983, *New York Times:* MOVE FOR IMPEACHMENT IS BEGUN BY SEVEN IN HOUSE
The issue: Seven members of Congress moved for impeachment following President Reagan's invasion of Grenada.

IMPEACHMENT!

IMPEACHMENT AND THE "PRESIDENTIAL-BOOGER FACTOR"

PRESIDENTS ARE SOMETIMES like boogers . . .get one on your finger (or in the White House) and it can be hard to shake it (or him) loose.

In the case of a booger, not even a few good swipes on your pantleg are guaranteed to remove the thing from the tip of your finger. And in the case of a president, not even a full-blown impeachment trial is guaranteed to remove the bum from his current perch at the White House.

Here's why:

Why Johnson got to stay in office after his impeachment:

Originally, the House filed eleven articles of impeachment against Johnson, but the Senate only voted on three of those charges. (The eleventh charge was a catchall that included the first ten charges.)

The Senate voted to acquit him rather than to convict him.

The final vote was thirty-five to convict, nineteen to acquit on all charges.

Since conviction required a two-thirds vote, Johnson missed being convicted by the Senate by a single vote.

Why Clinton got to stay in office after his impeachment:

President Clinton was tried in the Senate on a charge of perjury and on a charge of obstruction of justice.

The Senate voted to acquit President Clinton on both charges.

The final vote on the perjury charge was forty-five to convict, fifty-five to acquit.

The final vote on the obstruction of justice charge was fifty to convict, fifty to acquit.

A two-thirds vote (or sixty-seven total votes) was required to convict President Clinton on either or both charges.

SO WHAT IS IMPEACHMENT, ANYWAY?

IT'S SUCH A great-sounding word, isn't it? After all, it's just got that "Throw the bum out!" sound to it.

But in fact, that's not what it means at all. "To impeach" simply means "to make an accusation against someone" or "to bring charges or accusations against a public official."

Meanwhile, the road from being "impeached" to "throwing the bum out!" is a long one:

PATHWAY TO IMPEACHMENT, STEP ONE:
OVER AT THE HOUSE OF REPRESENTATIVES

- IN ARTICLE I, SECTION 2 OF THE U.S. CONSTITUTION, THE HOUSE OF REPRESENTATIVES IS GRANTED THE "SOLE POWER OF IMPEACHMENT."
- SO IT BEGINS IN THE HOUSE AND, ALTHOUGH THE CONSTITUTION DOESN'T SPECIFY HOW TO GET STARTED, THE PROCESS USUALLY BEGINS IN THE HOUSE JUDICIARY COMMITTEE. THE COMMITTEE STARTS WITH AN INVESTIGATION OF THE CHARGES AGAINST THE OFFICIAL (FOR OUR PURPOSES HERE, WE'RE TALKING ABOUT THE PRESIDENT, BUT AS YOU WILL SEE, OTHER OFFICIALS CAN BE IMPEACHED AS WELL).
- IF, AFTER HOLDING HEARINGS, THE JUDICIARY COMMITTEE'S FINDINGS SUGGEST THAT THE CHARGES ARE CORRECT, THEN THE COMMITTEE DRAFTS A RESOLUTION OF IMPEACHMENT, WHICH INCLUDES THE "ARTICLES OF IMPEACHMENT," AND SENDS IT ON TO THE REST OF THE HOUSE. IF, ON THE OTHER HAND, THE COMMITTEE FINDS THAT IMPEACHMENT ISN'T WARRANTED, IT DRAFTS A RESOLUTION THAT SAYS SO AND SENDS THAT ON TO THE FULL HOUSE.
- EVERY MEMBER OF THE HOUSE NOW VOTES ON THE RESOLUTION. IF THE HOUSE "ADOPTS" (OR "PASSES") ANY OF THE ITEMS ON THE "ARTICLES OF IMPEACHMENT" LIST (AND EACH ITEM ONLY HAS TO PASS BY A SIMPLE MAJORITY OF THE VOTES), THEN IT'S OFFICIAL—THE PERSON IS REGARDED AS "IMPEACHED" AND THEIR FATE NOW LIES IN THE HANDS OF THE U.S. SENATE.

IMPEACHMENT!

PATHWAY TO IMPEACHMENT, STEP TWO:
DOWN AT THE SENATE BUILDING

- ONCE AGAIN, THE U.S. CONSTITUTION PROVIDES THE DIRECTIONS. ARTICLE I, SECTION 3 TELLS US THAT "THE SENATE SHALL HAVE THE SOLE POWER TO TRY ALL IMPEACHMENTS." SO THE SENATE GOES TO WORK CONSIDERING WHAT JUST HAPPENED IN THE HOUSE.

- IF IT IS THE PRESIDENT WHO IS ON TRIAL, THE CONSTITUTION STATES THAT THE CHIEF JUSTICE OF THE SUPREME COURT WILL PRESIDE OVER THE TRIAL IN THE SENATE.

- CERTAIN MEMBERS OF THE HOUSE OF REPRESENTATIVES HEAD OVER TO THE SENATE BUILDING AND FUNCTION AS PROSECUTORS (THEY ARE CALLED "MANAGERS") AS THE SENATE TRIAL KICKS OFF. THE MANAGERS ARE EITHER CHOSEN BY THE SPEAKER OF THE HOUSE OR BY BALLOT, AND THE GROUP INCLUDES MEMBERS FROM BOTH PARTIES.

- JUST AS IN A COURT OF LAW, THE IMPEACHED PERSON'S LAWYERS PRESENT THE PERSON'S DEFENSE, AND THE LAWYERS ALSO HAVE THE RIGHT CROSS-EXAMINE WITNESSES.

- THE FULL SENATE ATTENDS AND OBSERVES THE PROCEEDINGS AS THOUGH THEY WERE A JURY IN A COURT ROOM.

- WHEN THE TRIAL CONCLUDES, THE MEMBERS OF THE SENATE MEET PRIVATELY TO TALK ABOUT A POSSIBLE VERDICT.

- THE SENATE THEN MEETS IN OPEN SESSION, AND THEY VOTE ON EACH "ARTICLE OF IMPEACHMENT." BUT THIS TIME, A TWO-THIRDS MARGIN IN THE VOTING IS REQUIRED IN ORDER FOR THE PERSON TO BE CONVICTED. IF NONE OF THE ARTICLES OF IMPEACHMENT IS APPROVED BY A TWO-THIRDS VOTE, THEN THE PERSON IS ACQUITTED.

- IF THE SENATE VOTES TO CONVICT, IT MAY THEN HOLD A SEPARATE VOTE TO REMOVE THE IMPEACHED OFFICIAL FROM OFFICE. THAT ISN'T REALLY NECESSARY, SINCE THE CONSTITUTION STIPULATES THAT FEDERAL OFFICIALS SHALL BE REMOVED FROM OFFICE UPON BEING IMPEACHED AND CONVICTED ANYWAY. BUT SINCE WE'VE NEVER BEEN DOWN THIS ROAD WITH A PRESIDENT BEFORE, THERE'S CURRENTLY BEEN NO PRECEDENT SET FOR WHETHER THIS SEPARATE VOTE SHOULD HAPPEN OR NOT!

WHITE HOUSE: CONFIDENTIAL

- IT'S INTERESTING TO NOTE THAT DURING AN IMPEACHMENT VOTE, THE VICE PRESIDENT MUST BE IN ATTENDANCE BUT DOES NOT IN THIS CASE ACT AS PRESIDING OFFICER. IF THE PRESIDENT IS CONVICTED, HE THEN LEAVES THE CHAMBER AND IS SWORN INTO OFFICE.

As you can see, the process of impeachment is pretty complicated. And there is plenty of evidence to suggest that the founders wanted it this way, simply because they intended it to be a last resort, and they didn't want the process to be so easy or so politicized that it could be used by one party against another or be used so frequently as to cause instability within the government as one leader after another was booted out of office.

IMPEACHMENT!

WE INTERRUPT THIS CHAPTER FOR AN ARGUMENT
AGAINST FREQUENT IMPEACHMENTS

"Impeachment, **like the atom bomb,**
is a weapon to be used only on very
rare and very special occasions."

—From an official U.S. government Web site

Here's the deal:

As we have all heard, politics makes strange bedfellows. But it also makes strange enemies. In other words, sometimes impeachment can be highly (or, let's face it, completely)
politically motivated.

Before you get all excited about throwing the current bum out (and we're speaking
hypothetically here, not about any particular bum), make sure you ask yourself and all your
political cronies the following questions . . . and answer them honestly:

1. Have you considered the consequences of having the instability of frequent impeach-
    ments as part of the country's regular political process?
2. Do you want to throw this guy out because he's not the guy you voted for, or do you
    want to throw him out because he's done something seriously wrong?

"An impeachable offense is whatever a majority of
the House considers it to be at any given moment
in history; conviction results from whatever
offense or offenses two-thirds of the other body
(the Senate) considers to be sufficiently serious to
require removal of the accused from office."

NAUGHTY PRESIDENT
OR NAUGHTY CONGRESS???

ONE OF THE trickiest parts of impeachment is trying to understand what kind of "bad behavior" can actually push a president over the line.

The authors of the Constitution wrote that grounds for impeachment included: "treason, bribery, or other high crimes and misdemeanors."

Treason, we understand.

Bribery, we understand.

But what are "high crimes and misdemeanors"?

And how do you differentiate between "high crimes and misdemeanors" and "We just found your political weak spot, and now we're going to pounce on it and exploit it"?

Congressman (and future president) Gerald Ford, arguing for his attempted impeachment of United States Supreme Court Associate Justice William O. Douglas in 1970 (this was the same Gerald Ford, by the way, who later pardoned Richard Nixon after Nixon resigned rather than go through an impeachment)

IMPEACHMENT STRATEGIES
THAT REALLY WORK

OPTION ONE: GET THE "IMPEACHMENT THING" OUT OF THE WAY BEFORE YOU BECOME PRESIDENT!

If a president absolutely *must* face a threat of impeachment at some point in his life, wouldn't it be great if he could face the problem *before* he actually becomes president?

That way, he isn't distracted by it while he's actually trying to be president!

And as strange as this idea may seem, it almost happened for one president.

Long before he was elected president, Thomas Jefferson served as the governor of Virginia. And one day in 1781, during Jefferson's last year as governor, the British invaded.

Jefferson chose to flee the scene on horseback and leave the invasion problem to the Virginia militia. His decision to run away probably saved his life, but there was one problem: As the governor, he was supposed to be in command of the militia!

Packing up and leaving was regarded as neglect of duty, and although the founding father was eventually exonerated, the Virginia House of Delegates demanded a full investigation of the matter, and for a brief time even contemplated impeaching the governor.

OPTION TWO: MISSED OUT ON THE "IMPEACHMENT THING" DURING YOUR PRESIDENCY? DON'T WORRY, YOU STILL MIGHT HAVE A SHOT AT IT LATER!

Even though his unpopularity as president led to him being voted out of office after one term, John Quincy Adams is the only president ever to be elected to the U.S. House of Representatives *after* his service in the White House.

This was an accomplishment in and of itself, but it seems that maybe Adams wanted something more to add to his political biography.

So during this "post-presidency" period of his life, he became intensely focused on highlighting how the South's desire for slavery and secession from the Union were threats to American liberty. He even baited Southern congressmen to get them to argue with him and attack him over the issue.

In fact, Adams became so nasty, and the debates he instigated became so intense, that at one point several Southern congressman contemplated the unthinkable—the possibility of IMPEACHING their own fellow congressman!

In the end, these Southern Representatives were unable to pull together the effort required to push an impeachment through, but for a brief period, Congressman Adams almost got to experience the kind of political fireworks he never managed to conjure up during his own presidency!

OPTION THREE: WHEN IN DOUBT, GO FOR "IMPEACHMENT LITE"

Considering how serious and complicated it is for the Congress to even begin a "formal inquiry" into the possibility of impeaching a president, you'd think there would be some other way a president can officially and formally be told: *Hey, stop acting like a jerk!*

And sure enough, there is:

ENTER THE "C" WORD: CENSURE

According to the Merriam-Webster Dictionary, the word *censure* means "a judgment involving condemnation"; it is also defined as "the act of blaming or condemning sternly" and "an official reprimand."

BAD BOY ANDREW JACKSON: A PRESIDENTIAL FIRST!

Eᴠᴇʀʏ ᴘʀᴇsɪᴅᴇɴᴛ ʜᴏᴘᴇs to do something really noteworthy, something really historic, during his time in office. But no president wants to be the first to have something really bad happen.

And despite his popularity and his successes in office, President Andrew Jackson has the dubious distinction of being the only president ever to be censured.

But by now the question you should've learned to ask is: Was this legit, or was it politically motivated?

We'll let you decide for yourself.

DOESN'T PLAY WELL WITH OTHERS, PART I: "OLD HICKORY" HAS PROBLEMS WITH A GUY NAMED HENRY

Andrew Jackson—nicknamed "Old Hickory" because he was such a tough guy—first ran for President in 1824 as one of five candidates. When the voting was finished, Jackson received a plurality (the most votes out of all the candidates) of the electoral votes, but not a clear majority (not more than 50 percent) of the electoral votes. With no clear majority, the next step in determining the winner was to do what the United States Constitution says to do in such cases—the names of the top three vote getters were given to the House of Representatives, and the reps were left to pick a winner.

To the surprise of many, the House picked John Quincy Adams to be the next president, and quickly after being declared the winner, Adams chose Henry Clay, a Congressman from Kentucky, to be his secretary of state. This outraged Jackson and his supporters so much that Jackson accused Adams and Clay of conspiring to do special favors for each other: if Clay would use his influence in the house of Representatives to sway votes to

Adams (which he did), Adams would give Clay a position in his administration (which he did).

So Adams won the election of 1824, and Jackson was, understandably, ticked off about it. And for the entire four years of the Adams presidency, Andrew Jackson and his fellow Democrats continually harassed the Adams administration with accusations of the so-called "corrupt bargain" between President Adams and Clay.

This not only made matters difficult for President Adams, but also created trouble for Henry Clay at the State Department. And the smear campaign was so effective that it helped lead Jackson to a huge victory over Adams in the presidential election of 1828.

DOESN'T PLAY WELL WITH OTHERS, PART II: "OLD HICKORY" GETS BACK AT 'OLE HENRY

After winning the 1828 election, Jackson quickly became an effective and incredibly popular president. When he began to make changes in Washington—like replacing longtime federal officeholders with appointees from his own party—Jackson claimed that he was getting rid of aristocrats and replacing them with "commoners." And he continued to make choices that reinforced his image of being a president who cared about everyday Americans.

But while "Old Hickory" seemed to be keeping American voters happy during his first term in office, he also seemed to be keeping an eye on Ol' Henry Clay. And Jackson would hold nothing back when he had an opportunity to do something that might really tick Clay off! For one thing, Jackson vetoed a bill that would have allowed federal assistance in the laying of a road in Clay's home state of Kentucky.

Meanwhile, something else began to brew in the Jackson administration that was even more disturbing to Clay. During his first term, President Jackson began working on a plan to put federal money in banks that were operated mostly by Democrat friends of his rather than putting the money where it had always gone in the past—in the more reliable Bank of the United States. This was viewed as reckless financial policy by Jackson's political foes.

IMPEACHMENT!

DOESN'T PLAY WELL WITH OTHERS, PART III:
HENRY'S REVENGE ON "KING ANDREW"

Clay was so eager to get at Jackson that he accepted the Republican Party's nomination for the presidency and tried to unseat Jackson in the election of 1832. Jackson won reelection quite handily, but Henry Clay still had a seat in the Senate and could still work to oppose Jackson's policies.

While Clay and others continued to sound the alarm about Jackson's reckless handling of federal money, members of Jackson's own administration began to question his policies as well. And Jackson had become so strong-headed that folks had begun to call him "King Andrew."

In the midst of a growing chorus of opposition, President Jackson had to contend with two Treasury secretaries who refused to go along with his plan to remove federal funds from the Bank of The United States. But Jackson wouldn't give up. In fact, to get his way he flat-out fired both Treasury secretaries — one right after the other!

When it appeared that nothing was going to change President Jackson's mind about his monetary policy, Senator Henry Clay got the ultimate revenge and gave his nemesis another historical title. Led by Clay in 1834, the Senate for the first time in history voted to censure the President of the United States, charging Andrew Jackson with "dictatorial and unconstitutional behavior."

For the next three years, Jackson and his friends worked night and day to wipe out any physical evidence of the censure from the Senate record, and they finally did by the time Jackson left office in early 1837. But despite these efforts, Andrew Jackson still holds the title of the only president to ever be censured.

Speaking of being "politically motivated," it's worth asking if Jackson was working so hard to get all

Note to Elvis, Michael Jackson, and Howard Stern: Back in the 1800s, calling someone "King" was quite an insult. After all, this new nation had just recently been born in revolt against the tyranny of a king!

federal funds out of the Bank of the United States because he thought it was the right thing to do or because he knew his enemy Henry Clay had helped start the bank back in 1816!

{ "I have only two regrets: that I have not shot Henry Clay or hanged J. C. Calhoun." }

Andrew Jackson (J. C. Calhoun was Jackson's vice president [until he resigned] and also a buddy of Henry Clay)

IMPEACHMENT!

WHAT IF COLONIAL-ERA AMERICANS HAD THEIR OWN BLOGS AND WEB SITES?

Have you noticed how easy it's been for us to Google the current president along with the words "impeachment" and "censure" and then include today's headlines from various newspapers right in this book?

This is, of course, the first time in history that we the people have had that kind of power at our fingertips.

In the past, getting the latest news from all corners of the nation took days or even weeks. Today, it takes about a minute.

BUT WHAT IF BLOGS AND THE WEB HAD EXISTED BACK IN THE DAYS OUR NATION WAS FOUNDED?

Chances are good that at any given time during our country's history, there has always been someone wanting to impeach the president. Let's face it—no matter how popular or successful a president is, he can't keep everyone happy all of the time. And for some people, the president is always a guy you love to hate—no matter who he is.

So imagine going back and re-visiting some of the issues that were brewing in the country in times past. Consider how people may have felt about the president in light of those issues. Certain presidents would seem to have been more likely targets of "impeachment talk" than others, simply because of their behavior in office or because of the problems that the country was facing at the time or both.

Now imagine past presidents having to deal with the kind of scrutiny faced by our two most recent presidents, George W. Bush and Bill Clinton. That is, imagine yesterday's presidents dealing with the instantaneous and continuous flow of ideas, facts, opinions, and, yes, rumors, that are available instantaneously today via the World Wide Web!

Granted, in times past there were far more newspapers in our country than there are today, and that provided lots of opportunity for all kinds of reporting and editorializing. But not everyone could own their own newspaper or immediately publish their own editorials.

But today, on the other hand, nearly anyone can operate their own Web site or blog. And this means that if you're angry at the president, you can instantly express your frustration with him to people all over the country, even around the world.

97

Newsflash!

Even as we sit here writing this chapter, the following headline appears at NewYorkTimes.com:

SENATOR SETS HEARING ON CENSURE OF BUSH

> " . . . there's word of mouth, there's blogs, there's Internet, there's all kinds of ways to communicate which is literally changing the way people are getting their information."
>
> President George W. Bush, March 22, 2006

IMPEACHMENT!

So just for fun, let's pretend it *wasn't* Vice President Al Gore who invented the Internet, but our very first vice president, John Adams, instead.

And then let's pretend that all presidents had to work under the scrutiny of a blogging media which could instantly report on their (perceived or politically spun) missteps or errors in judgment. Herewith we present the bloggable offenses of presidents past:

George Washington **"the world will be puzzled to decide whether you are an apostate or an imposter,** whether you have abandoned good principles, or whether you ever had any." (Thomas Paine, 1796)

James Madison **President Declares War!**
He asked Congress to declare war on Britain—which led to the British invasion and the burning of Washington two years later.

James Monroe **"It's the economy, stupid!"**
An economic depression set in two years after he took office, and of course many blamed him for it.

{ "You are perfectly insane and should apply for admission to the Lunatic Asylum. . . . You are a curse to the Whig Party and to the nation." }

A would-be blogger sends a love-note to John Quincy Adams

John Quincy Adams **First Faux President???**
He was the first president to win election with a majority of the electoral college vote but a minority of the popular vote (sound familiar?), which for some people was reason enough to be ticked off at him. His ideas about spending tax dollars on roads, canals, and scientific exploration were also very unpopular.

Andrew Jackson **Early-American Bloggers: "Impeach this bum!"**
He was popular with most Americans. However, his plan to put federal money in banks managed by his buddies rather than in the Bank of the United States had lots of people muttering about impeachment and led to his being the first president to be "censured."

Martin Van Buren **"It's STILL the economy, stupid!"**
Marty, Marty, Marty . . . weren't you paying attention while James Monroe was in office? If you had been, you would have known that being president during an economic depression is no way to win a popularity contest, and you would have done anything to avoid yet another one.

John Tyler **Second Faux President???**
He was the first person to become president without technically being elected to the office (he assumed the presidency from the vice presidency when President William Henry Harrison died a month after being inaugurated), which left a lot of people angry and saying "he's not the *real* president!" Even without a bunch of bloggers competing to coin the most clever phrase, he still got tagged with the nickname "His Accidency.

Zachary Taylor **Duh! He kept forgetting to get out the vote**
He was a war veteran who had never even voted in a presidential election before he was elected, and he got caught in the middle of the debate over slavery between the North and the South and had people on both sides of the issue very angry; then he died suddenly during his second year as president.

Abraham Lincoln **See "13 OTHER IMPEACHMENTS THAT GOT AWAY" on page 80.**

IMPEACHMENT!

Andrew Johnson	**He really was impeached!**
	He tried to move forward with Lincoln's plans for reconstructing the South and ended up becoming the first president to be impeached (see "Impeachment: The Real Deal #1" on page 103).
Ulysses S. Grant	**"Grant-Gate?"**
	He was a war hero–turned–president, but because of his lack of political experience, he seemed to have no clue about how to *be* president, and dishonest associates took advantage of him constantly. Fraud and scandal pervaded his administration, and by the end of his second term Americans were glad to see him go—and he was glad to be gone.
Rutherford B. Hayes	See "13 OTHER IMPEACHMENTS THAT GOT AWAY" on page 80.
Chester Arthur	**P. O.'d his own party**
	Another Veep who became president without being elected president, he actually wanted people seeking jobs in the civil service to pass a competency exam that was pertinent to the job they were pursuing—which really ticked off his Republican buddies, who had helped him climb the political ladder. The Republican Party bigwigs were so angry, in fact, they refused to nominate him for a second term.
Theodore Roosevelt	**"Try and impeach me . . . I dare ya!"**
	Despite being a popular president who won reelection unanimously, he ticked off members of Congress because he seized the Isthmus of Panama without Congressional approval and moved forward to build the Panama Canal, all on his own. He actually spoke of his own impeachment, saying: "I regard the Senate as a collection of angleworms. If they don't like my leadership they can impeach me."

William Howard Taft	See "13 OTHER IMPEACHMENTS THAT GOT AWAY" on page 81.
Woodrow Wilson	See "13 OTHER IMPEACHMENTS THAT GOT AWAY" on page 81.
Herbert Hoover	See "13 OTHER IMPEACHMENTS THAT GOT AWAY" on page 81.
FDR	See "13 OTHER IMPEACHMENTS THAT GOT AWAY" on page 82. Then look again.
Harry Truman	See "13 OTHER IMPEACHMENTS THAT GOT AWAY" on page 82. Then look again. And again. And again. And again.
JFK	**Begged to be blogged** As you read in an earlier chapter, this was a guy with a social life that was just BEGGING to be blogged. And of course, bloggers continue to blog about his assassination to this day.
LBJ	See "13 OTHER IMPEACHMENTS THAT GOT AWAY" on page 83.

"Blogs"?

You may be interested to know that the first president to ever publicly say the word *blog* during a speech was George W. Bush.

For what it's worth, President Bill Clinton was the first president to send an e-mail.

Bill Clinton was also the first president to play a saxophone on a late-night TV talk show, *The Arsenio Hall Show* . . . which was one of those shows that President George Herbert Walker Bush called "weird talk shows" during the 1992 presidential campaign.

Richard M. Nixon	Can you say "Watergate"?
Gerald Ford	Can you say "Presidential pardon"?
Jimmy Carter	**Economy in the tank! Iranian Hostage Crisis!!** The Iranian Embassy hostage crisis started on his watch and, amazingly enough, ended just a few hours after Carter left office and Ronald Reagan replaced him. Meanwhile, the economy slid into the tank and interest rates soared to over 20 percent.
Ronald Reagan	**See "13 OTHER IMPEACHMENTS THAT GOT AWAY" on page 83.** Oh, and let's not forget about Iran-Contra.
George H. W. Bush	You didn't think we were going to forget about Iran-Contra, did you?
Bill Clinton	Can you say "Monica Lewinsky"?
George W. Bush	Did we mention this headline over at WashingtonPost.com:

"Democrats Are Split
As Impeachment Whispers Get Louder"

IMPEACHMENT: THE REAL DEAL #1!

AFTER THE CIVIL War—and after President Lincoln's assassination—the big task facing the country and the new president, Andrew Johnson, was Reconstruction, the process of putting the country back together after it had been divided so severely. And there were two different theories in Washington about how to accomplish this:

- One theory suggested that the states cannot be destroyed by the acts of their own people, and state sovereignty cannot be handed over to the national government. Basically, this meant that the individual states were pretty much responsible for themselves, and the only job that the federal government had to do was to try and calm things down—to "quiet the riots," so to speak—and to try and create a situation were things could get "back to normal."
- The other theory of reconstruction viewed the Civil War as a struggle between two separate governments. This meant that since the South lost the war, the Southern states were now "conquered territories," and therefore the federal government of the United States could pretty much do whatever it wanted with them. In other words, the Southern states could be admitted back into the Union—or not!—depending on how folks in Washington felt about it.

With the American people so horribly divided on how they viewed their own country, it was difficult to imagine how any one president could lead them all.

JOHNSON TAKES A STAND . . . AND IT'S ALMOST HIS LAST

President Johnson was definitely a believer in the first theory, which meant that he presumed that the South was still a part of the United States.

But there was more at stake in the division between the two theories than just land. The folks from the North, advocates of the "conquered territories" idea, also believed in the full political equality of the recently freed slaves. The Southerners, on the other hand, wanted more limited rights for the freed slaves—and this created even more contention between the North and South, *and* between President Johnson and the Congress.

So, while the Republican majority in Washington wanted the Southern states admitted back into the Union *if* they agreed to change their ways regarding the freed slaves, President Johnson and the Southern Democrats wanted to make sure that the Union was actually "unified," even if that meant that the Southern states held on to some of their old, segregationist ways.

The Republican Congress tried to legislate their plans for the Southern states, President Johnson vetoed them, and the Congress managed to override him on one occasion. But through it all there was very little "unity" in the Union—which meant trouble for the country, for Reconstruction, *and* for President Johnson.

IMPEACHMENT, DOUBT, AND DISILLUSIONMENT . . . IN THAT ORDER

By February of 1868, Andrew Johnson was almost finished with his term as president, and he had little or no hope of being nominated for a second one. And while members of the House had begun talking about impeaching him, many outside the halls of government doubted that there was any value in impeaching a president who would be leaving office so soon anyway. Horace Greely, Editor of the *New York Tribune,* asked bluntly:

"Why hang a man who is bent on hanging himself?"

Still, there were those in Washington who believed that impeachment was the right thing. These were primarily the Republican members of the Congress, who led the House to pass articles of impeachment on February 24, 1868. And while many members of the Northern states' press initially favored impeaching Johnson, some began to change their minds once they arrived in Washington and observed firsthand what was actually going on.

Famed Civil War–era newspaper correspondent George Alfred Townsend described the Senate trial of President Johnson as "a more terrible scene than the trial of Judas Iscariot might be before the College of Cardinals."

He also observed that about the only folks who were truly upset with Johnson were Congressman Thaddeus Stevens and Senator Charles Sumner—two members of Congress who were driving forces in the impeachment effort.

THE PARTY LINES ARE CROSSED, AND A PRESIDENCY IS SAVED . . . BUT JUST BARELY

While impeachment-bent Republicans in the Congress continued to publicly express confidence in what they were doing, privately they began to doubt that they would be successful. And despite the fact that the Republicans held more than a two-thirds majority in the Senate, when it came time to vote to impeach the president—which it did on May 16th of 1868—seven Republicans broke ranks with their party and voted to acquit the president on impeachment charges, fearing that to impeach Johnson would permanently damage the office itself.

Johnson then served out his term and left the White House in March of 1869, only to return to Washington six years later to serve in the U.S. Senate.

IMPEACHMENT: THE REAL DEAL #2!

W E'RE NOT GOING to bore you with endless details about the Clinton (and we should be specific and say we're talking about *Bill* Clinton, since his wife Hillary now has a job from which *she* can be impeached as well) impeachment. After all, you were there. You lived through it.

But for many Americans, the debate continues as to whether or not President Clinton should have been convicted of impeachment charges and, frankly, whether or not he should have been impeached in the first place.

Many who believe the Clinton impeachment was wrong still say that to cheat on one's spouse is not an "impeachable offense," while others who think impeaching President Clinton was the right thing will say "The problem was not adultery, but perjury (intentionally lying under sworn oath)."

No doubt you've got your own opinion. And you're entitled to it. (And if you're wondering why we're being uncharacteristically quiet about this, then it's time to go back and reread our second disclaimer at the beginning of this book.)

RICHARD NIXON AND THE "ALMOST IMPEACHMENT"

RICHARD NIXON WAS the first president ever to resign . . . but to be fair, he was a president of "firsts," both good and bad.

For example, he is the first and only person to have been elected twice to the vice presidency and twice to the presidency.

His presidency was also marked by several diplomatic accomplishments, including "détente"—an official "relaxing of tensions" between the United States and the former Soviet Union—and the official U.S. recognition of the Chinese government.

But unfortunately, Nixon was also involved in a bunch of illegal activity—which included bribery, blackmail, and obstruction of justice. And most all of this illegal stuff—the stuff that brought down his presidency—was centered around the scandal known as "Watergate."

While Nixon won a landslide reelection victory in 1972 and didn't resign from office until 1974, the investigation that led to impeachment charges and his resignation surrounded events that dated back to his earliest years in office.

NIXON'S FIRST PRESIDENTIAL TERM: THE GROUNDWORK FOR IMPEACHMENT

Although few realized it at the time, the dirty tricks of the Nixon administration started long before Watergate:

June 13, 1971—The Defense Department's secret history of the Vietnam War, aka the "Pentagon Papers," is published by the *New York Times*.

September 3, 1971—The so-called "White House plumbers unit," a group of guys that got its name because it was given orders to "plug leaks" in the administration, executes a break-in at a psychiatrist's office to search for information on Daniel Ellsberg, the former defense analyst who leaked the Pentagon Papers.

$\Big\{$ "Get a good night's sleep and don't bug anybody without asking me." $\Big\}$

—President Richard Nixon

June 17, 1972—Five guys, one of whom claims that he used to work for the CIA, are arrested at 2:30 in the morning while trying to bug the offices of the Democratic National Committee at the now-famous Watergate Hotel.

June 19, 1972—The *Washington Post* reports that a Republican Party aide is one of the Watergate burglars. Former attorney general John Mitchell, now heading up the Nixon reelection campaign, denies a link between the party and the break-in.

August 1, 1972—Reports emerge claiming that a $25,000 cashier's check, intended for the Nixon re-election campaign, somehow ended up in the bank account of a Watergate burglar.

September 29, 1972—Rumors begin to swirl suggesting that Former Attorney General John Mitchell once controlled a secret Republican fund used to finance widespread intelligence-gathering operations on Democrats.

October 10, 1972—Reports begin to surface claiming that FBI agents have established that the break-in at the Watergate Hotel was associated with the Nixon reelection campaign and part of a large-scale political spying and sabotage effort.

November 7, 1972—Nixon wins big-time! He is reelected to his second term in one of the largest landslides in American presidential history, winning more than 60 percent of the vote and winning forty-nine states in the Electoral College against Senator George McGovern of South Dakota, his Democratic opponent.

NIXON'S SECOND TERM: THINGS BEGIN TO LOOK GRIM

Despite the fact that some "questionable stuff" had already come to light during Nixon's first term in office, Americans overwhelmingly entrusted the White House to him for another four years. But not long after his second inauguration, things really started to get ugly—and the "questionable stuff" that emerged during his first four years in office began to look more and more like the "stuff" that impeachment is made of.

April 30, 1973—H. R. Haldeman and John Ehrlichman, two "major players" in the White House, resign from their respective jobs because of the Watergate scandal, along with U.S. Attorney General Richard Kleindienst. White House counsel John Dean also gets the boot.

May 18, 1973—The Watergate channel! The Senate Watergate Committee begins investigative hearings, which are covered on national television. Attorney General–designate Elliot Richardson retains former solicitor general Archibald Cox to serve as the Justice Department's "special prosecutor."

{"I am not a crook."}

—President Richard Nixon

June 3, 1973—Reports surface indicating that former White House counsel John Dean has admitted that he discussed the Watergate cover-up with President Nixon at least thirty-five times.

June 13, 1973—News breaks of a memo that was discovered by Watergate prosecutors. The memo, addressed to John Ehrlichman, describes in detail the plans to break into the office of Daniel Ellsberg's psychiatrist.

July 13, 1973—Uh-oh, there are tape-recordings of all this stuff! Former presidential appointments secretary Alexander Butterfield reveals in congressional testimony that Nixon recorded all conversations and telephone calls in his offices since 1971.

IMPEACHMENT!

> "I'm glad I'm not Brezhnev. Being the Russian leader in the Kremlin, you never know if someone's tape recording what you say."
>
> —President Richard Nixon

July 18, 1973—It is reported that Nixon demanded that his White House taping system be disconnected.

July 23, 1973—Nixon refuses to turn over his presidential tape recordings to the Senate Watergate Committee or the special prosecutor.

October 20, 1973—*Saturday Night Massacre!* Archibald Cox is canned, and the office of the special prosecutor is shut down—all at the hands of President Richard Nixon. Attorney General Elliot Richardson and Deputy Attorney General William D. Ruckelshaus resign. And talk in the Congress about impeachment is heating up.

December 7, 1973—The White House can't explain why there is an 18½-minute gap on one of Nixon's subpoenaed tapes. Nixon's Chief of Staff, Alexander Haig, suggests that "some sinister force" has erased it. *(Nice try, Al.)*

April 30, 1974—The White House hands over more than twelve hundred pages of edited transcripts of President Nixon's tapes to the House Judiciary Committee. The Committee, however, demands that the tapes themselves must be released.

July 24, 1974—In a unanimous ruling, the United States Supreme Court rejects Nixon's claims of "executive privilege," and determines that he must hand over the tape recordings of sixty-four specific White House conversations.

July 27, 1974—The House Judiciary Committee passes the first of three articles of impeachment, charging the president with "obstruction of justice." It appears that the full House would be inclined to pass it as well.

August 8, 1974—Richard M. Nixon makes history (again) by becoming the first U.S. president to resign from office.

WHITE HOUSE: CONFIDENTIAL

"People in the media say they
must look at the president with a
microscope. Now, I don't mind a
microscope, but boy, when they use
a proctoscope, that's going too far."

—President Richard Nixon

FIFTEEN OTHER IMPEACHMENTS
(AND ONE RECALL)
YOU MIGHT WANT TO KNOW ABOUT:

1

Year:	1797
Accused:	Senator William Blount of Tennessee
The story:	He was impeached by the House for trying to chase the Spanish out of Florida and Louisiana using a combination of Indians, frontiersmen, and the British navy. In the end, the bulk of the land was to go to Britain with the remainder going to Tennessee. The case was later dismissed by the Senate in 1799 when it was ruled that a U.S. Senator could NOT be impeached.
What happened:	*Dismissed*

2

Year:	1803
Accused:	U.S. District Court Judge John Pickering of New Hampshire
The story:	He was impeached for drunkenness, loose morals, and practicing unlawful judicial procedures. In the end, he was convicted by the Senate and removed from office.
What happened:	*Convicted, removed from office*

③

Year:	1804
Accused:	Samuel Chase, Associate Justice of the Supreme Court
The story:	Some say it was all a plot by Thomas Jefferson to remove Federalist judges from the bench, but in the end Chase was impeached by the House but acquitted by the Senate.
What happened:	*Acquitted*

④

Year:	1830
Accused:	Judge James H. Peck of the U.S. District Court of Missouri
The story:	He was impeached by the House for abusing his judicial powers, but he was acquitted by the Senate.
What happened:	*Acquitted*

⑤

Year:	1862
Accused:	Judge West Hughes Humphreys of the U.S. District Court of Tennessee
The story:	He was impeached by the House, convicted by the Senate, and removed from office for supporting the South's secession from the Union and for then accepting a judicial position as a judge with the Confederacy.
What happened:	*Convicted, removed from office, became Confederate judge*

IMPEACHMENT!

6

Year:	1873
Accused:	Judge Mark Delahay, U.S. District Court Judge of Kansas
The story:	He resigned before the House could impeach him on charges of drunkenness, among other things.
What happened:	*Resigned*

7

Year:	1876
Accused:	William Belknap, Secretary of War
The story:	He was charged with taking money in exchange for making a military appointment. He resigned from office and was acquitted by the Senate.
What happened:	*Resigned, then acquitted*

8

Year:	1904
Accused:	Judge Charles Swayne, U.S. District Court of Florida
What happened:	He was impeached by the House for submitting false expense accounts, among other things. In the end he was acquitted by the Senate.
The story:	*Acquitted*

9

The year:	1912
Accused:	Judge Robert W. Archbald, U.S. District Court of Pennsylvania
The story:	He was impeached by the House and convicted by the Senate for using his position to strong-arm railroads into giving him sweetheart deals on coal-rich land.
What happened:	*Convicted*

Year:	1926
Accused:	Judge George W. English, U.S. District Court of Illinois
The story:	He was impeached by the House for doing things like threatening jurors with jail time if they didn't vote to convict a defendant and also for summoning local and state officials to his courtroom and for berating them in public using obscene language; he resigned before the Senate could vote on his case
What happened:	*Resigned before Senate could vote*

Year:	1933
Accused:	Judge Harold Lounderback, U.S. District Court of California
The story:	He was impeached by the House for using his office for financial gain but was acquitted by the Senate.
What happened:	*Acquitted*

⑫

Year:	1936
Accused:	Judge Halsted Ritter, U.S. District Court of Florida
The story:	He was impeached by the House and convicted and removed from office by the Senate for income-tax evasion.
What happened:	*Convicted, removed from office*

IMPEACHMENT!

Year:	1986
Accused:	Judge Harry Claiborne, U.S. District Court of Nevada
The story:	He was impeached by the House and convicted and removed from office by the Senate for income-tax evasion.
What happened:	*Convicted, removed from office*

Year:	1989
Accused:	Judge Walter L. Nixon, U.S. District Court of Mississippi
The story:	He was impeached by the House and convicted and removed from office by the Senate on charges of perjury.
What happened:	*Convicted, removed from office*

IMPEACHMENT #15

(AND OUR PERSONAL FAVORITE BECAUSE IT HAS A HAPPY ENDING)

IMPEACHED BY THE HOUSE,
CONVICTED BY THE SENATE,
ELECTED TO THE HOUSE

In 1988, U.S. District Court of Florida Judge Alcee L. Hastings was impeached by the House and convicted and removed from office by the Senate for accepting a bribe, for making false statements during a trial, and for disclosing confidential info from an FBI wiretap.

During the impeachment and afterward, ex-Judge Hastings never wavered from his "Not guilty!" plea.

> "I am not guilty of having committed any crime. . . . And that is my defense . . . and will remain until I die, my defense."
>
> —Alcee L. Hastings, defending himself before a full Senate chamber in 1989

As you might expect, Hastings, the son of domestic workers, was devastated by his conviction and removal from office.

In addition to the disgrace of the impeachment, he was also unemployed and deep in debt. In fact, he had even borrowed $13,000 from his mother's retirement account to defend himself.

Yet just a few years later in 1992, as Hastings continued to insist that he was innocent, he ran for and won a seat in the U.S. House of Representatives, and to this day he continues to serve in the House with many of the same House members who voted to impeach him in the late 1980s.

IMPEACHMENT!

AND ONE RECALL:

It was a glitzy, glamorous Kennedy spouse versus a very gray politician named Grey.

The party line was that Grey (Gray?) needed to be recalled because he'd mishandled the state budget and mishandled the state's electricity crisis.

On the other side, there were charges of things being mishandled, too, but we'll save those specific accusations for the "Sex!" chapter in the next edition of this book, after Arnold gets himself elected president.

But please allow us to say that anyone who really expected Gray (Grey?) Davis to defeat Arnold Schwarzenegger in an election clearly was not paying attention to the premise of this book . . .

. . . which is that that when you get down to it, politics is all about entertainment.

And with that in mind, is it any wonder that since the recall Arnold Schwarzenegger and Gray Davis have become good friends? After all, Arnold now has Gray's old job as governor, and he could surely use some pointers. But even more importantly, Gray is now dying to get Arnold's old job as an actor. Since the recall, in fact, he's been constantly pestering his new buddy Arnold for acting tips.

118

5
Fights!

"**S**HAKE HANDS AND say you're sorry."

It's what every dad says to every son after said son has gotten into a fight. And when you're six or eight or twelve, it actually works.

By the time you get to be president, however, things are all blown out of proportion. It's just not that easy anymore. There's that run for reelection, after all. There's saving face. There's ego and power and political machismo at stake.

So you get into a political skirmish, and you kill off a reputation. You get into a battle of ideologies, and you kill off a long-standing friendship. Or you go completely off the deep end and kill the man, your opponent, altogether.

Hey, you're president—leader of the Western world. Killing off your opponent, therefore, is all in a day's work.

GETTING AWAY WITH MURDER!
(THE VICE-PRESIDENTIAL WAY)

Lᴇᴛ's ꜱᴀʏ ʏᴏᴜ'ʀᴇ vice president and minding your own business when one day along comes Alexander Hamilton, calling you "despicable" and "dangerous" to your face—what do you do?

If you're Aaron Burr, vice president under Thomas Jefferson, you challenge him to a duel and then swiftly kill him.

Ahh, but *now* what to do?

Let's learn again from Burr. He was charged with murder in New York (where Hamilton actually died) and charged and indicted in New Jersey (where the duel occurred). He might have done what Spiro Agnew did more than a century and a half later, which was to claim that a sitting vice president had the protection of executive privilege and therefore could not be indicted. Instead Burr did a far more brilliant thing: He returned to Washington D.C. and resumed his duties as vice president and president of the Senate as if nothing had happened. Burr knew he was safe since neither New York nor New Jersey had any jurisdiction in Washington D.C. and thus couldn't extradite him.

NOT THE END OF BURR

Remarkably, Burr was allowed to finish out his term. As the term ended he began to concoct a grand scheme that would allow him not only to get away with the murder of Hamilton but also to involve a group of coconspirators who would help him grab parts of the Louisiana and Orleans Territories.

Why? He planned to create and rule an empire that would stretch far into Mexico.

By anyone's definition, what Burr planned was treasonous (not to mention insane), and when Thomas Jefferson got wind of it, he called for Burr's arrest.

By now Burr's life was pretty complicated. First, he was wanted for murder. Second, he was wanted for treason. Third, he found out it was one of his own coconspirators who tipped President Jefferson off to the plan.

So he did the only reasonable thing; he turned himself in. Again he was indicted. This time he stood trial. And miraculously, he was acquitted when Chief Justice John Marshall ruled that one could only be found guilty of an act of treason if the act had been attested to by at least two witnesses.

Again Burr made a wise move: He left the country and didn't return until 1812.

{ There is nothing I love as much as a good fight. }

—FDR

"I SHOT HIM, SIR": PART ONE

Dick Cheney, of course, made history on February 11, 2006, for being the first U.S. vice president since Aaron Burr to point a gun at another man and pull the trigger.

In Cheney's case, the incident was a hunting accident. But Cheney's early response to the shooting was much like Burr's: After shooting his hunting partner, seventy-eight-year-old Harry Whittington, Dick Cheney went back to work in Washington without making any sort of statement to the press about what happened.

"I SHOT HIM, SIR": PART TWO

Burr wasn't the only one fighting duels. By some accounts, Andrew Jackson was involved in more than a hundred of them—most to defend the honor of his wife, Rachel.

In fact, Jackson was a walking armory: He had a bullet in his chest from an 1806 duel and another in his arm from a barroom fight in 1813.

The barroom shooter was Missouri senator Thomas Hart Benton. When Jackson was elected to the Senate, the two sat side by side and became close friends. Or as Benton said, "General Jackson was a great man. I shot him, Sir" and "Yes, I had a fight with Jackson. A fellow was hardly in the fashion who didn't."

"I 'TONGED' HIM, SIR"

James Monroe once got so angry at his secretary of treasury that he chased him out of the White House with a pair of red-hot fire tongs.

On another day, when President Monroe invited the ministers of both Britain and France over to the White House for dinner, things didn't quite work out as planned. In fact, relations got so heated between the two ministers that they got into a fight, and both had their swords drawn before Monroe could break them apart.

RICHARD NIXON:
MEANER THAN A JUNKYARD DOG

WELL, HE MAY not have had a .32-caliber gun in his pocket or a razor in his shoe, but politically Richard Nixon was every bit as bad as "Bad, Bad Leroy Brown," and he was always getting into fights just like a mean old junkyard dog.

It all started when he was thirty-two and responded to a classified ad in his local newspaper. It was an ad placed by local Republicans; they were holding a talent search for a young veteran who leaned to the right but who had no political experience.

Their goal? To enter the young man into the race for a local seat in the House of Representatives, which had been held by the same Democrat for ten years.

NIXON AS A LIGHTWEIGHT

Nixon took to politicking like a piranha. When his wealthy Republican supporters told him to attack, he went straight for his opponent's throat, stretching the truth to make it look like the incumbent—who had recently been named Best Congressman West of the Mississippi by a group of Washington journalists—actually had the support of a communist group.

It was a brilliant strategy on two counts. First, Nixon's opponent was caught off guard and forced to defend himself against mostly baseless negative charges. Second, even if the incumbent had wanted to retaliate with a negative campaign of his own, Nixon had no political history upon which to draw.

Nixon won by 67,874 votes to 49,431, and his political modus operandi was set.

NIXON AS A WELTERWEIGHT

The next time Nixon stepped into the ring, he was a member of the House Un-American Activities Committee and his opponent was Algier Hiss. Nixon rose to national

FIGHTS!

prominence as a result of the Hiss case and was easily reelected to the House of Representatives.

While the Hiss case was for many years a source of great controversy, today historians and political scientists generally agree that Hiss was, in fact, a communist.

NIXON AS A MIDDLEWEIGHT

It was time for Nixon to run for the Senate. His opponent was incumbent Helen Gahagan Douglas, who had held the seat for four years. It was during this battle that Nixon won the nickname "Tricky Dick." He won the election (and the nickname) by labeling Helen Douglas the "pink lady" and issuing propaganda listing the number of times she and a known communist House member from New York had cast the same votes. While it was true Congresswoman Douglas had voted the same as the communist congressman Marcantonio as many as 354 times, Nixon neglected to mention in his propaganda that he himself had voted the same as Marcantonio 112 times, as had many of his fellow Republicans.

Regardless of the morality of Nixon's charges, they worked, and he won his way into the Senate while also making a name for himself in Washington and nationally.

Years later, when asked about his smear campaign against Congresswoman Douglas, Nixon replied, "I'm sorry about that episode. I was a very young man."

NIXON AS A JUNIOR HEAVYWEIGHT

Nixon's next opponent was the press—and he was becoming a smart boxer, learning how to communicate directly with the voter.

When Ike was nominated for president by the Republicans in 1952, Nixon was his first choice for running mate. Nixon, after all, was the perfect foil for Eisenhower's squeaky-clean, paternal image.

Then the trouble began. The *New York Post* ran a story headlined "SECRET NIXON FUND." The story reported that Nixon had a secret eighteen-thousand-dollar slush fund he used to pay for expenses. The story was enough to kill Nixon's career—and given the way he had campaigned in the past, he had a lot of enemies who would have loved to exploit the story. And that was just the Democrats. On the Republican side there were also many who wanted to see Ike drop Nixon from the ticket.

Ike, however, kept a cool head. If Nixon could prove himself innocent and clear his name, Ike said, then he could remain on the ticket. And Ike was more than pleasantly surprised with the result of the flap, for Nixon not only cleared his name but also generated a flood of phone calls and letters to the Republican National Committee demanding he be allowed to remain on the ticket.

Here's how Nixon turned the tide: He used seventy-five thousand dollars of the Repub-lican National Committee's money to speak on national television for thirty minutes about his eighteen-thousand-dollar secret fund. In his speech he exposed the "facts" behind his personal finances: He and his wife, Pat, had a two-year-old Oldsmobile and owned a small amount of equity in their homes in California and Washington D.C. but had no other real assets like stocks or bonds.

> "If I'm a traitor, the United States is in a helluva shape."
>
> —Harry Truman, upon finding he was the focus of one of Nixon's communist witch-hunts

Then Nixon really laid it on strong. "Pat doesn't have a mink coat," he said, "but she does have a respectable Republican cloth coat. And I always tell her she'd look good in anything."

Finally, Nixon's confession:

> A man down in Texas heard Pat on the radio mention the fact that our two youngsters would like to have a dog and, believe it or not, the day before we left on this campaign we got a message from Union Station in Washington that they had a package for us. We went down to get it. You know what it was? It was a little cocker spaniel in a crate that had been sent all the way from Texas— black and white, spotted, and our little girl Tricia, the six-year-old, named it

Checkers. And you know, the kids, like all kids, loved the dog, and I just want to say this right now, that regardless of what they say about it, we are going to keep it.

Thus Nixon won the hearts and votes of America . . . and Ike. When Nixon and the general met the next day, Eisenhower greeted Nixon with a handshake, a grin, and the words: "You're my boy."

In spite of his success it should be noted that Nixon at no time during his speech attempted to explain the eighteen-thousand-dollar slush fund.

Checkers, Anyone?

Checkers, by the way, died in 1964 and is buried at the Bide-A-Wee Pet Cemetery on Long Island outside New York City—although there is a movement afoot by the Nixon Library to have him exhumed and reburied next to the president in Yorba Linda, California.

NIXON TAKES HIS FIRST LOSS . . .
AND HIS NEXT . . . AND HIS NEXT . . .

Following his successful runs for the vice presidency as Ike's running mate in 1952 and 1956, Nixon lost his bid for the presidency to Kennedy in 1960. Next he ran for governor of California against incumbent Pat Brown in 1962—and lost. And he lost his battle against the press when he held a press conference on the day after his defeat in the governor's race and announced: **"This is my last news conference. . . . You won't have Dick Nixon to kick around any more."**

FINALLY: NIXON AS "HEEEEAVYWEIGHT
CHAAAAMPIIIION OF THE WOOOORLD"

Imagine you are visiting a good friend after a long spell has passed. The last time you stopped by, about four years earlier, your friend's eight-year-old son was nothing but trouble; he constantly demanded attention by whatever means it took to get it. He was loud and rude and relentless.

Today, as you stare at the polite, well-spoken twelve-year-old young man before you, you ask yourself, *Is this really the same boy?*

Like a little boy who had finally grown up, Richard Nixon shed his shrill, combative shell and became a man who was in control of himself and the world around him. Instead of acting like an attack dog, he began acting like a statesman. Instead of hunting communists, he became a strong proponent of detente with the Soviet Union and a rapprochement with the Communist government of China. This led to the beginning of the Strategic Arms Limitation Talks (SALT) with the Soviets. And in 1972 he traveled to both China and Russia and became the first U.S. president ever to visit either of these countries.

Nixon's first term was not all rosy, however—the escalation of the Vietnam War cost many lives and caused great strife and havoc at home.

THE NEW NIXON FALLS APART

Call it paranoia or call it fear of failure . . . or give it some other name copped from the annals of pop psychology, but the burglary, the coverup, and the tapes (missing as well as accounted for)—the string of events most of us call *Watergate*—were all executed in vain. By most accounts Nixon was already a shoo-in for reelection, even without the "dirty tricks."

PRESIDENT TRUMAN PICKS A FIGHT

MARGARET TRUMAN, HARRY'S daughter, once tried her hand at being a professional singer—but she sure didn't get much praise from the press.

At least one critic, however, found out that criticizing the daughter of the president can be a tricky business. After Paul Hume of the *Washington Post* gave Margaret a negative review he got a letter from her father, the president, warning him that if they ever met he would need "a new nose and plenty of beefsteak."

"HEY, HEY, LBJ: HOW MANY FRIENDS DID YOU MAKE TODAY?"

FROM ALFRED STEINBERG'S book *Sam Johnson's Boy,* we learn of this exchange in 1956 between Senate majority leader LBJ and *Newsweek* reporter Sam Shaffer:

> "If you want to know what Lyndon Baines Johnson was going to do at the national convention," Johnson screamed, "why didn't you come to Lyndon Baines Johnson and ask him what Lyndon Baines Johnson was going to do?"
>
> "All right," said Shaffer, hiding all signs of intimidation, "What is Lyndon Baines Johnson going to do at the convention?"
>
> "I don't know," was the answer.

"Why do you come and ask me,
the leader of the Western world,
a chicken-shit question like that?"

—LBJ, in response to a reporter's question
he obviously deemed trivial

FORTUNATELY, ACTIONS
SPEAK LOUDER THAN WORDS

As you may recall, when running for president the first time, George W. Bush campaigned on a theme of "civility" and often spoke of "changing the tone in Washington."

Which struck some people as odd after a microphone caught him making the following remark to running mate Dick Cheney at a planned campaign stop near Chicago while the crowd cheered, a marching band played in the background, and George and Dick just kept waving, waving, waving to the large crowd of adoring supporters:

"There's Adam Clymer, major league asshole from the *New York Times*."

To which Dick Cheney simply replied, with all the civility and tone-changing attitude he could muster:

"Yeah . . . big time."

FIGHTS!

TEDDY AND TAFT: A LOVE STORY

THEY HAD ONCE been the best of friends. In fact, while Teddy Roosevelt was in office, he groomed William Howard Taft to replace him.

When joined by a third friend, Elihu Root, they called themselves "The Three Musketeers." Teddy Roosevelt was D'Artagnan (of course), Taft was Porthos, and Elihu Root was Athos. In reality these three men were perhaps the most powerful men in the world, for Roosevelt was president, while Taft and Root were his secretaries of war and state respectively.

Roosevelt and Taft were an unlikely pair of friends. Roosevelt was a man of action, a wound-up cyclotron of energy and excitement, a rugged outdoorsman and soldier who met life head-on and was always headed out the door for a new and grand adventure. Taft, on the other hand, was large (sometimes weighing as much as 330 pounds) and slow-moving and required so much sleep that his closest aide had learned to cough loudly and wake him when he nodded off during meetings.

Perhaps it was Roosevelt's secret in life, but he always brought out the best in the people around him. His influence over Taft provides the perfect example of this. Taft found Teddy's attention and trust to be flattering and confidence-boosting. He became, you might say, a new man, for he was always eager to please, and here now was a man to serve who was so much larger than life—you could even say Teddy was much larger than Taft himself. With Roosevelt solidly behind him, Taft was easily elected president. However, once in office Taft discovered that no matter how large his feet were, it was not so easy to fill the presidential shoes of Theodore Roosevelt—and when he

Mr. Taft Writes a Letter

- "When I am addressed as 'Mr. President' I turn to see whether you are not at my elbow."
- "I want you to know that I do nothing in the Executive Office without considering what you would do under the same circumstances."
- "I can never forget that the power that I now exercise was a voluntary transfer from you to me."

turned to ask Roosevelt for help, the former president was gone, off to Africa on safari and on other far-flung adventures.

Taft made some mistakes. He did some things that displeased his old friend Teddy. And by the time Teddy Roosevelt returned to the States, the damage was done. From Roosevelt's perspective, Taft had turned his back on what he—as president—had begun. Their friendship ended both bitterly and publicly.

Taft was devastated by the loss. In truth, he had never wanted to be president. He had only pursued the office to please his ambitious wife, who wanted to be First Lady, and to help his friend Teddy continue to carry out the policies they both believed in.

Meanwhile, an angry Roosevelt decided to run against his former friend for the Republican nomination when it came time for Taft to run for reelection.

The fight for the party's support was bitter, leaving the two ex-friends calling each other names like "weakling," "puzzlewit," and "fathead with the brains of a guinea pig" (Roosevelt of Taft) and "egotist" and "demagogue" (Taft of Roosevelt). Taft eventually won the Republican Party's nomination, while Roosevelt started his own party to run against him. Ironically, neither won, for the Republican Party split the vote and Democrat Woodrow Wilson won with 41.8 percent of the vote. Roosevelt took second with 27.4 percent, and Taft took third with 23.2 percent.

Taft, of course, was the real loser in more ways than one. Not only had he lost the election, but he had also lost the friend who had helped him grow from cocoon to butterfly.

YEARS LATER, A HUG AND A HANDSHAKE

Five years later, while checking into Chicago's Blackstone Hotel, Taft was informed by a clerk that Theodore Roosevelt was at that moment upstairs in the restaurant dining alone. Taft made his way to the dining room immediately and, according to William Manners's *TR and Will:*

> Looking about, Taft finally located TR at a little table across the room and walked quickly toward him. Intent on his meal though TR was, the sudden

stillness in the dining room caused him to look up. He immediately threw down his napkin and rose, his hand extended. They shook hands vigorously and slapped each other on the back. Those in the dining hall cheered, and it was not until then that TR and Will Taft realized that they had an audience and bowed and smiled to it. Then they sat down and chatted for a half hour.

As we say today, closure is a wonderful thing. And for Teddy and Taft, time was of the essence, for Roosevelt died less than a year later.

Taft later expressed his feelings about their reconciliation meeting:

> I want to say to you how glad I am that Theodore and I came together after that long painful interval. Had he died in a hostile state of mind toward me, I would have mourned the fact all my life. I loved him always and cherish his memory.

What color was Taft's parachute?

After serving as president, Taft went on to the Supreme Court, even becoming chief justice. Ironically, this was really the job he had always wanted; he only ran for president to please Teddy and his own ambitious wife.

As Taft himself once said, "Next to my wife and children, [the Court] is the nearest thing to my heart." And "The truth is that in my present life [as chief justice] I don't remember that I was ever president."

6
Money!

CONSIDER THIS:

> Only one president in our nation's history
>
> —Andrew Jackson—
>
> ever paid off the national debt.

GREED! CORRUPTION! GRAFT!

IT'S A PROBLEM.

On an almost consistent basis over time, those presidents who campaigned the longest and hardest to end corruption in government had the most corrupt administrations.

"Why would that be?" you ask?

Theories abound. One suggests that those who scream the loudest about corruption are probably the most corrupt. Others postulate that the presidents who went down in history for having corrupt administrations are those who devoted the most to rooting the corruption out.

INTRODUCING THE KING OF CORRUPTION

THE THREE PRESIDENTS who made the biggest stink about government corruption were probably Buchanan, Grant, and Truman. Ironically, they also had three of the most corrupt administrations in history.

To be fair, no one has ever pointed a finger at Harry Truman or Ulysses S. Grant and accused them personally of any wrongdoing. In both cases they were upright and honest guys who made the same mistake: They appointed their good buddies from back home to key positions in their administrations—but their buddies were neither qualified to hold those jobs, nor did they bring to their jobs the strong moral backbone needed to serve their country without serving themselves (quite liberally and profitably) first.

Corrupt? No. Just stupid.

Chester A. Arthur once sold twenty-six
wagonloads of White House furniture
for a total of eight thousand dollars.
What he apparently didn't know was
that some of the furniture was priceless.

BUCHANAN, ON THE OTHER HAND, WAS A SNAKE

{
"Next in importance to the maintenance of the Constitution and the Union is the duty of preserving the government free from the taint, or even the suspicion, of corruption."
}

—from the inauguration speech of James Buchanan

EVEN BEFORE HE was elected:

- Buchanan promised lucrative government contracts to friends in exchange for large campaign contributions.
- Supporters in some states arranged for aliens to be illegally naturalized and then transported to the polls.

And after he was elected:

- Buchanan promised to award handsome contracts to a contributor who gave $16,000 to his campaign.
- A large navy contract was given to a company in Philadelphia that promised to influence the reelection of a close friend of Buchanan's.
- Giant printing contracts were given to another close friend, who then subcontracted them at half the price to printers who made large contributions to the president's election campaign. Printing contracts were also used to twist the arms of various members

How bad could it get, you ask?

James Buchanan's administration was so corrupt that given a chance to buy Cuba for only thirty million dollars, Congress voted to pass on the deal because there was a collective fear that Buchanan and his cronies would somehow abscond with the money.

of Congress—if members voted with the president, the large contracts would be awarded to printers in their states or districts.

- The postmaster of New York embezzled $155,000 and fled the country.
- The secretary of war resigned after bilking the government of five million dollars.
- The personal banker of the secretary of war won the right to buy a military reservation in Minnesota.
- The House doorkeeper was found guilty of falsifying accounts and had to resign.

"THAT'S WHAT FRIENDS ARE FOR"

WHETHER YOU ARE talking about Buchanan or Grant or Truman, the finger always gets pointed at the same place: their friends.

Grant and Truman, however, existed on a much higher moral plane. While it's true they made the mistake of putting their no-good friends in high places, they didn't know their friends would repay them by robbing the country blind.

Buchanan, on the other hand, knew exactly what was going on. In fact, in one case Buchanan received a letter suggesting he give a lucrative navy contract to a particular company in Philadelphia that in return promised to help influence the congressional reelection of one of Buchanan's close friends. Buchanan initialed the letter, sent it to the Navy Department, and the Philadelphia firm was awarded the contract.

Ten days later Buchanan's friend won reelection.

Disclaimer: Any similarities between the historical events detailed above and more recent events is purely ironic.

NOT EVEN QUICKEN COULD HELP

As Ulysses S. Grant's presidency showed, he was not terribly good with money. But he was a war hero, and he did have a good name, and that was worth something. After he left the White House, he became a partner in the investment house of Grant & Ward—which subsequently failed and left him in debt. Although he had cancer at the time, he put pen to paper and wrote his memoirs to pay off his creditors.

While the book was a huge success and earned more than $450,000, Grant died four days after he finished writing it.

Bringing New Meaning to the Phrase "Pay Pal"

Harding's administration was overrun with corruption as well, but at least he never got on a soapbox about it before taking office. Like Truman and Grant, it was his friends who were on the take, not Harding himself. In fact, when he died, he was deeply in debt.

"IT'S THE ECONOMY, STUPID"

LET'S FACE IT, dealing with money is half the job. Chances are that's why Jimmy Carter didn't get reelected.

And, short of getting lucky, there's only one way to win the money game when you're president: You've got to have great financial advisers.

The funny thing about Carter is that if he wanted good economic advice, he didn't have to look any further than his own daughter. After all, while he was running for president in 1976, she set herself up with her own booming business right on the lawn of the Georgia governor's mansion.

Had Jimmy used the same simple techniques to run the government that Amy used out on the lawn, the country might not have been saddled with skyrocketing inflation and prime interest rates in the range of 20 percent during his term in office.

But at least, we presume, Carter is doing better with his own finances—unlike Thomas Jefferson, James Monroe, Andrew Jackson, Ulysses S. Grant, and Warren Harding. All four of these guys were so bad at managing their own money they died poor and (with the exception of Jefferson) in debt.

DID AMY CARTER LEARN ABOUT
$$$ FROM LBJ?

LYNDON JOHNSON MADE his first foray into the world of business when he opened Johnson's Shoe Shine Shop inside Cecil Maddox's barbershop. For the first few weeks the business ran fine, in part thanks to Cecil's existing customer base and the ads LBJ ran in the local paper. But then disaster struck: LBJ's father shut the business down because he didn't think it was any way for a nine-year-old to spend his time.

While her father was running for president, Amy Carter was outside with friends selling lemonade to tourists and members of the press. Initially, the price was a nickel, but Amy soon realized the market could bear a price increase.

So she raised the price to a dime. Yet business was still booming, so the three young entrepreneurs expanded and added new products to their line: three varieties of sandwiches and Frisbee rentals. The business was suddenly closed, however, when the Secret Service declared it a potential security risk.

143

FOR LOVE OR MONEY

WHILE A YOUNG man, JFK appeared at a rally for candidates who were running for the Massachusetts legislature. He waited patiently as candidate after candidate went before the audience and spoke—and he noticed a similarity in the stories each of them told.

When his turn finally came to address the assembly he began: "I seem to be the only person here tonight who didn't come up the hard way!"

While life for Kennedy was relatively easy in his younger years, the same was not true for all of our presidents. Some, in fact, had to do some pretty odd things to make ends meet before making it into the Oval Office.

President:	**George Washington**
Job:	During his first year as president, he ran a ferry service back and forth across the Potomac.
President:	**Thomas Jefferson**
Job:	Given a choice, he once said, he would have rather been a gardener than president. He imported plants from other countries to study them, and while conventional wisdom of the time said tomatoes were poisonous, he grew and ate them for dinner. He was also an inventor and was responsible for the development of the dumb waiter, the lazy Susan, an automatic closing door the design of which is still—fundamentally—in use on buses today, the revolving chair, the folding chair, and a machine that enabled him to make a duplicate copy of a letter as he wrote it. He was also an inventive chef and created both Baked Alaska and Chicken à la King (which George Washington loved!).

President:	**John Quincy Adams**
Job:	Okay, he didn't exactly come up the hard way, either, but at age fourteen he was made private secretary to the American envoy to Russia, and at fifteen he was secretary to the American emissaries negotiating peace with England. In addition, he is the only president to be a published poet.
President:	**Zachary Taylor**
Job:	He was a career military man. Before being elected president he spent most of his adult life fighting Indians and the Mexican army during the Mexican-American War. Funny thing was, he was a very short war hero, so he needed someone to give him a boost every time he got up on his horse.
President:	**James Buchanan**
Job:	He was once a prizefighter.
President:	**Grover Cleveland**
Job:	In the span of just three and a half years he was the mayor of Buffalo, New York, the governor of the state of New York, and the president of the United States. Before becoming mayor of Buffalo, he was the sheriff of Erie County, New York, and was called upon twice to spring the trap at a hanging—thus making him the only president in history with the job of hangman on his résumé.
President:	**William McKinley**
Job:	He drove a coffee wagon out to soldiers on the battlefield during the Civil War. His commanding officer was Rutherford B. Hayes.

145

MONEY!

President:	**Teddy Roosevelt**
Job:	He spent several years working as a cowboy in the Dakota Badlands—and after he rounded up a gang of rustlers, he wore the badge of a deputy sheriff.
President:	**Warren G. Harding**
Job:	He was a newspaper man . . . and a poker player. In fact, he won controlling interest in the *Marion Daily Star,* his local newspaper, in a card game.

{ As Harding used to say at his weekly poker game: "Forget that I'm president of the United States. I'm Warren Harding, playing poker with friends, and I'm going to beat hell out of them." (And when he was short of cash, he would ante up by putting pieces of White House china into the pot.) }

President:	**Herbert Hoover**
Job:	Hoover was an orphan, and his first job was picking bugs off potato plants—for which he was paid a dollar per hundred (bugs, that is, not plants).

His first job out of college was as a mine worker—for seventy hours a week he pushed an ore cart in a California gold mine. Using what he learned while getting a degree in mining engineering from Stanford, he went on to become a millionaire.

But everything Hoover touched didn't turn to gold. In fact, he aspired to be a political writer and wrote many books containing his views and commentary on the state of the world . . . that no one wanted to read.

On the other hand, he did write two books that did rather well. The |

first, which he wrote twenty-one years before he became president, was called *Principles of Mining*. In fact, it became the definitive text for mining engineering students until it went out of print almost sixty years later. His second success as an author? It was *Fishing for Fun and to Wash Your Soul*, which he wrote thirty-three years after leaving the White House.

President: **Harry Truman**

Job: After World War I, he opened a haberdashery in Kansas City with a friend. Three years later they were broke.

President: **LBJ**

Job: He worked on a road gang after high school. Later, he put himself through college by working as the college janitor and picking up trash on campus.

President: **Richard Nixon**

Job: He spent his summers working as a carnival barker for the Wheel of Chance at the Slippery Gulch Rodeo. Later, he owned the only hamburger stand in the South Pacific, Nixon's Snack Shack, during World War II.

147

{ "I have often thought that if there had been a good rap group around in those days, I would have chosen a career in music instead of politics." }

—Richard Nixon

President: **Jimmy Carter**

Job: Flew blimps for the navy.

MONEY!

President:	**Gerald Ford**
Job:	As a college senior he was recruited to play for the Detroit Lions and the Green Bay Packers—but he decided to go to law school instead. While at Yale Law School, he worked as an assistant football coach, a boxing instructor, and a magazine model. He also worked as a forest ranger at Yellowstone National Park. His chief duties: directing traffic and feeding the bears.
President:	**Ronald Reagan**
Job:	According to Reagan, he saved the lives of seventy-seven people as a boy when he worked as lifeguard at the river near his family home in Dixon, Illinois.
President:	**George H. W. Bush**
Job:	His first job after he left the navy was on the Texas oilfields. His responsibilities included painting machinery and sweeping floors.
President:	**Bill Clinton**
Job:	Clinton's first boss was his grandfather, who owned Cassidy's General Store in Hope, Arkansas. Bill's job was to greet customers with a smile and a hearty handshake as they came through the door of the store.
President:	**George W. Bush**
Job:	In between his years as an undergraduate at Yale and getting his MBA at Harvard, he worked as a social worker tutoring underprivileged children.

Presidents who were never lawyers or never studied the law:

- George Washington
- William Henry Harrison
- Zachary Taylor
- Ulysses S. Grant
- Woodrow Wilson
- Warren G. Harding
- Herbert Hoover
- Dwight Eisenhower
- JFK
- LBJ
- Jimmy Carter
- Ronald Reagan
- George H. W. Bush
- George W. Bush (he tried, but he was rejected by the University of Texas Law School)

DOES CRIME PAY?

AFTER GERALD FORD granted Richard Nixon a full pardon for any crimes he may have committed in relationship to Watergate, he then lobbied Congress to pay Nixon $850,000 to cover his expenses while making the transition from the presidency to civilian life.

The sum of $850,000 was considered to be a compromise deal since The Presidential Transition Act of 1963 provides ex-presidents who complete their full term in office with one million dollars to cover their expenses during this six-month transition period.

In a compromise deal of its own, Congress agreed to pay Nixon two hundred thousand dollars for his transition expenses.

MONEY!

A FEW GOOD MEN . . .

- George Washington refused to accept his salary as president.
- Herbert Hoover and JFK both took the money and donated it to charity.
- When Eddie Cantor and the Lone Ranger asked the children of America to each send a dime to the president to help the March of Dimes—of which FDR was the founder and chairman—so many dimes were sent to the White House (sometimes as many as 150,000 a day) that fifty extra postal workers had to be hired to handle the increased volume. In total, more than three million dimes were received.

. . . ONE STINKER . . .

In 1991 *Spy* magazine reported that it cost the Secret Service three million dollars a year to protect the life of former President Gerald Ford and that the government was also spending $420,000 a year to maintain his office.

Meanwhile, Ford was leveraging his role as chief executive for every dollar he could get.

Consider this: When Ford turned the White House over to Jimmy Carter in 1977, his net worth was about $250,000. Just a few years later, after allowing a variety of companies ranging from American Express to Commercial Credit to Spectradyne (the company that pumps pay-per-view movies, including porn, into many hotels) buy him for as much as $140,000 a year each, he was a millionaire.

Okay, "buy him" is a bit harsh. Let's say they paid him to be a consultant or a member of the board of directors. He got the dough (as much as $1.7 million a year in the late 1980s)—they got the prestige. So, to the degree that Ford is still cutting these kinds of deals, he now supports himself the same way Michael Jordan does.

Not a bad deal for a guy who was appointed vice president when Spiro Agnew resigned, who succeeded to the presidency when Richard Nixon resigned, and who then lost to Jimmy Carter when he ran for reelection. (In other words, unless you're from his home state of Michigan, this is one president you never had a chance to elect.)

But here's the rub: In 1993 Congress voted to stop funding the offices of former presidents by 1998, although they'll still receive an annual pension equal to that of a cabinet secretary (currently $183,500/year) and Secret Service protection for life.

Ford, however, who made a fortune by lending his name and presidential status to a myriad of corporate sponsors who could afford to pay for it, lobbied Congress hard to push that cutoff date further into the future so he could stay on the U.S. government gravytrain as long as humanly possible.

. . . AND ONE GUY WHO WASN'T TOO BRIGHT

James Monroe entered politics at the age of twenty-four and worked in public service for the rest of his life. He was a member of the Virginia Assembly and the Continental Congress, a senator, a minister to France, the governor of Virginia, secretary of state, and president for two terms. He was a man truly devoted to his country.

Only one problem: For many of the forty-nine years he spent as a public servant, he spent more than he earned. Therefore, when he retired in 1825 after his second term as president, he was broke. So he did the only logical thing: He turned to the government for a handout.

His rationale was that if he served his country for close to fifty years and had less money than he started with, then much of the money he spent on the expenses of being a public servant must have been his own. Therefore, didn't it seem reasonable that he should be reimbursed?

It took them seven years to do it, but Congress finally reimbursed Monroe thirty thousand dollars—just a fraction of what Monroe claimed to have spent. Not that it mattered. By the time Congress made the decision, Monroe had sold off all his land to pay his debts and had gone to live with his daughter and son-in-law. He died shortly afterward.

151

MONEY!

"JUST PUT IT IN YOUR POCKET!"

For what it's worth, presidential salaries through the ages:

1789–1873

George Washington through
the first term of Ulysses S. Grant $25,000/year

1873–1909

Grant's second term through
the final term of Teddy Roosevelt $55,000/year

1909–1949

William Howard Taft's term through
Harry Truman's first term . . . . $75,000/year (taxable)

1949–1969

Harry Truman's second term through
LBJ's final term . . . . $100,000/year (taxable)

1969–2001

Richard Nixon's first term
to Clinton's second term . . . . $200,000/year (taxable)

2001–present

George W. Bush's first term
through present . . . . $400,000/year (taxable)

The office also comes with certain perks:

- You don't ever have to make your own bed.
- You don't ever have to cook your own breakfast (although that was something Gerald Ford liked to do anyway).
- You don't ever have to do your own laundry or take your own clothes to the dry cleaner (but you do have to pay for the dry cleaning yourself; you will be billed for it at the beginning of each month).

SURPRISE!

The following also come free with the job:

- ballpoint pens
- personalized stationary
- high-speed Internet access
- toothbrush cups emblazoned with the presidential seal
- nightly bedspread turn-down service
- breath mints

ANOTHER SURPRISE!

You have to pay for your own:

- food (although you may be able to defray some of these costs with various expense accounts)
- clothes
- haircuts and manicures
- toothpaste, hairspray, razor blades

MONEY!

His Just Reward

Isn't it an amazing coincidence that FDR was the chairman of the March of Dimes and also happens to be pictured on the dime?

No coincidence at all, as it turns out. In fact, after FDR died in 1945, Congress voted to commemorate the work he did on behalf of the March of Dimes by putting his profile on the coin.

THE **BEST** SURPRISE!

In addition to your $400,000/year salary, you also get:

- a no-questions-asked $50,000 expense account—in other words, you're not required to provide receipts to get reimbursed.
- to live rent-free in a nice big house that includes a bowling alley, putting green, jogging track, billiard room, tennis courts, swimming pool, and movie theater (with various contacts in Hollywood providing all first-run movies for free).
- five full-time chefs who are standing by to prepare the food you paid for (see above).
- a nice, secluded, 180-acre vacation home in Maryland called Camp David that includes numerous cabins for the president and guests, a heated pool, tennis, horseshoes, bowling, a three-hole golf course, an archery range, and a trout stream.
- the presidential version of "public" transportation: limos, helicopters, and your own personal jets.
- up to one million dollars you can spend every year for "unanticipated needs," in case you ever go over budget somewhere else.

7

Prophecy!

"If anybody really wanted to shoot the president
of the United States, it is not a very difficult job—
all one has to do is get on a high building some
day with a telescopic rifle and there is nothing
anyone can do to defend against such an attempt."

— JFK, three hours before he was assassinated

MORE KENNEDY PROPHECY

- Senator William J. Fulbright once said to JFK, "Dallas is a very dangerous place. I wouldn't go there. Don't you go."
- JFK's favorite poem was "I Have a Rendevous with Death" by Alan Seeger.
- One of Jackie Kennedy's first jobs out of college was as the *Washington Times-Herald*'s "Inquiring Photographer." Below are three of the questions she asked Washington celebrities, politicians, and people on the street:

If you had a date with Marilyn Monroe, what would you talk about?

Should a candidate's wife campaign with her husband?

What prominent person's death affected you most?

WEIRD LINCOLN PROPHECY

{
"You will win the election and will be elected for a second term.
But I fear . . . you may not survive your second four years
in the White House."
}

—Mary Todd Lincoln to her husband, after he was nominated for
president for the first time but before he was elected

- Abraham Lincoln was the first president ever to be photographed at his inauguration. Eerily, in one photo he stands near the man who would later assassinate him, John Wilkes Booth.
- Abe Lincoln's young son Robert was waiting for a train one day when the crowd on the platform surged forward to meet the incoming train. Robert lost his footing and began to slip between the platform and the moving train . . . until a hand reached out and grabbed him, saving his life. The helping hand belonged to the famous actor Edwin Wilkes Booth. Unbeknown to Booth or the young boy whose life he just saved, Booth's brother would later shoot and kill the boy's father.
- Robert Lincoln is the only man in the history of the United States known to have witnessed the assassinations of three different presidents—his father, Abraham Lincoln; James Garfield; and William McKinley. After he saw anarchist Leon Czolgosz shoot McKinley, Robert Lincoln vowed he would never again appear in public with an incumbent president.

"I believe there are men who want to take my life. And I have no doubt they will do it."

—Abraham Lincoln, hours before he was shot

"It has been advertized that we will be there and I cannot disappoint the people. Otherwise I would not go. I do not want to go. Good-bye, Crook."

—Abe's last words to White House guard Colonel William Crook

(Lincoln's last two words confused Crook until later in the evening when he heard the president had been shot; the president's customary salutation to Crook when he was going out for the evening was "Good night.")

"They won't think anything of it."

—Abraham Lincoln's last words, in response to Mrs. Lincoln's question as to whether he thought the audience at Ford's Theatre would mind if they held hands while watching the performance

WHITE HOUSE: CONFIDENTIAL

PRESIDENTIAL DESTINY

THERE GOES LIFE imitating art again.

At one point Ronald Reagan was considered for the role of Rick in the film *Casablanca* (translation: "white house"). And before they were married, he and Nancy Reagan appeared in the General Electric Theatre production of *A Turkey for President*.

William Henry Harrison promised voters that if elected he wouldn't run for another term. How prophetic—he died thirty-one days after taking office.

LBJ started telling people he was going to be president when he was in the first grade. His first real presidential experience was his election to the office of president of his high school senior class. Whether or not he won the election on merit can be argued, however—it turns out no one else in his graduating class of six wanted the job.

When Dwight D. Eisenhower and his brother, Edgar, graduated high school, their yearbook predicted Edgar would grow up to be president of the United States—and Dwight would someday be a history teacher.

159

{ "I wish for you that you may never be president." }

—Grover Cleveland to
five-year-old FDR

PROPHECY!

"HOW CAN YOU ARGUE WITH THAT?"

RICHARD NIXON WAS a high school and college debate champion. In fact, his team at Whittier College once won twenty-seven straight matches.

"He was so good it kind of disturbed me," his debate coach once remarked. "He had this ability to kind of slide around an argument, instead of meeting it head-on."

MORE NIXON PROPHECY

A young Nixon once remarked to his mother, "Mother, I would like to become a lawyer—an honest lawyer, one who can't be bought by crooks."

For her part, Hannah Nixon said of her son Richard that he was the "best potato masher a mother could wish for."

"The convention will be deadlocked, and after the other candidates have gone their limit, some twelve or fifteen men, worn out and bleary-eyed for lack of sleep, will sit down, about two o'clock in the morning, around a table in a smoke-filled room in some hotel, and decide the nomination. When that time comes, Harding will be selected."

—A frighteningly accurate prediction by Warren Harding's campaign manager, Harry Daugherty

CONGRESS AND THE PRESIDENCY:
THE DAY THE LOVE AFFAIR ENDED

TODAY, AS WE all know, the Senate has one hundred members, but when George Washington was president, the Senate was a small, intimate group of just twenty-six.

This made it easy for all of the members and the president to have a close, conversational relationship.

But keep in mind that despite the warm reception George always got when he visited the Senate, the Constitution is also quite clear about the separation of powers between the Executive and Legislative branches. And George found out exactly what this meant on the day he appeared before the twenty-six Senators, as he had always done, and made his pitch about the bill he wanted them to sign, as he had always done.

Unlike all his previous encounters with the Senate, on this day, the members did not rush to give him the vote he wanted.

Instead, they squirmed and fidgeted and stared at their shoes . . . while George stood before them in uncomfortable silence.

Then, finally, one Senator explained to the President that it was their right to discuss the bill *in private* before voting on it. At which time a stunned George Washington took the hint and headed for the door.

PROPHECY!

"I CHANGED MY MIND"

While Harry Truman was president, it became obvious the White House needed major renovation work done after Harry, and the bathtub in which he was soaking, almost fell through the floor and into the middle of a reception Bess was holding for the Daughters of the American Revolution.

While it was true the house did need a new foundation, reinforced beams, steel framing, fireproofing, air conditioning, and the latest in communications technology, it was Truman's idea to add a balcony to the second floor of the South Portico so he and his family and their guests could sit outside and enjoy Washington's evening breezes.

Truman, however, didn't anticipate the expense of the balcony project or the controversy and problems the addition would create, especially for the Treasury Department. After all, there were millions of twenty-dollar bills in circulation that showed the White House without a balcony, and what on earth were they going to do about that?

But Truman put his foot down, got his way, and got his balcony. He and his family moved out of the White House for twenty-seven months, living across the street at Blair House while the executive mansion could be gutted and rebuilt.

Here's the punchline of the story: *Two days after the White House project was complete, Harry Truman announced he wouldn't seek reelection.*

LINCOLN-KENNEDY COINCIDENCES?

YOU'VE HEARD THEM before:

- Both had seven letters in their last names, both were over six feet tall, and both were athletic.
- Both were shot in the head on a Friday, and both were seated beside their wives when shot.
- Lincoln was shot at Ford's Theatre, and Kennedy was shot in a Lincoln limo, which is made by Ford.
- Lincoln was in Box 7 at Ford's Theatre, and Kennedy was in Car 7 of the Dallas motorcade.
- In both cases, the assassin had three names with fifteen letters: John Wilkes Booth and Lee Harvey Oswald.
- Booth shot Lincoln in a theater and was captured at a warehouse. Oswald shot Kennedy from a warehouse and was captured in a theater.
- Kennedy's secretary, Evelyn Lincoln (whose husband's nickname was Abe), told him not to go to Dallas. Some say Lincoln had a secretary named John Kennedy who told him not to go to the theater.
- Both were elected to the U.S. House of Representatives for the first time in '46, were runners-up for their party's nomination for vice president in '56, and were elected president in '60.
- Both were succeeded by southern Democrats named Johnson.

163

PROPHECY!

The list goes on and on, and it's interesting stuff, but so what? They both had two hands, two feet, and two eyes too. They both put on their pants one foot at a time, and they both . . . well, you get the idea.

The bottom line of the Lincoln-Kennedy coincidences is this: You can think about them all day long, and all you'll have at dinner time is a creepy feeling and an urge to watch *X-Files* reruns all night.

On the other hand, if you take the time to delve into the not-so-eerie similarities between the Kennedy and Adams (as in John and John Quincy) families, you might just learn something about yourself, your own family, and even the world around you. And that, in our opinion, is a day's work worth doing.

"Just as I went into politics because Joe [Jr.] died, if anything happened to me tomorrow, my brother Bobby would run for my seat in the Senate. And if Bobby died, Teddy would take over for him."

—JFK

"The world is tired of us."

—Brooks Adams, great-grandson of John Adams

WHAT ABOUT THE ADAMS-BUSH COINCIDENCES?

1. Only two men who have been president have ever had a son become president: President John Adams was the father of President John Q. Adams, and President George Bush is the father of President George W. Bush.
2. The sons of both presidents had the same first name as their fathers, the presidents.
3. Both sons ran against candidates from Tennessee: John Q. Adams ran against Tennessee Senator Andrew Jackson, and George W. Bush ran against Vice President (and former Tennessee Senator) Al Gore.
4. And both sons lost the popular vote to their Tennessee opponent . . . but still became president: despite losing the popular vote, John Q. Adams was elected by the House of Representatives; despite losing the popular vote, George W. Bush was elected by the Electoral College.

THE INFAMOUS KENNEDY FAMILY

Joseph (Joe) Patrick Kennedy Sr. was one of the richest men in the country in the '20s and '30s. First he was a bank president. Tiring of that, he went to Hollywood to make movies (and have an affair with Gloria Swanson). Tiring of that, he moved on to become FDR's chairman of the Securities and Exchange Commission (SEC) and then ambassador to England. At this point, he began to have his own aspirations toward the presidency. His dream, however, was thwarted as FDR ran for a third and fourth term. That was when Joe Kennedy decided if he couldn't be president, at least one of his sons would be.

JOE KENNEDY SENIOR HAD FOUR SONS

Joe Jr. was the heir apparent of his father's wish to be president. The elder Kennedy pushed all of his sons to play hard, to ignore pain and risk and danger, and to win at all costs—but he pushed Joe Jr. the hardest. Joe Jr., after all, had the toughest job of all ahead of him: winning the presidency. Tragically, after flying fifty missions as a navy pilot during World War II and receiving his orders home, Joe Jr. volunteered to fly one last mission as the pilot of an experimental airplane. The plane exploded in midair, and Joe Jr.'s body was never found. Why did he agree to that final flight—one that was acknowledged to be dangerous—when he could have been on his way home instead? Some have suggested that he was driven by the fierce competitive spirit instilled in him by his father. After all, his younger brother John (JFK) had already won a Purple Heart.

John Fitzgerald inherited his father's dream. And with JFK, Joe Sr. finally realized that dream. However, we all know the ending to that chapter: After winning the presidency in 1960, JFK was assassinated in 1963.

Robert was JFK's attorney general and had just won the California Democratic Party's presidential primary for the 1968 election when he was assassinated. Like his brother John, he seemed to relish taking risks—even after his brother was assassinated, he ignored the warnings of friends and family and even the Secret Service and would rush out into crowds unprotected.

Ted was the only one left. Many predicted he would win the Democratic Party's nomination for president in 1972 . . . until he drove his car off the side of a bridge, managed to free himself, claimed to have dived back down into the water to save his passenger, then went on to the party they had been headed to to get help. He did not call the police until the next day.

It was assumed that Bobby or Ted would eventually capture the presidency again for the Kennedy clan, and if not one of them, then one of the next generation's sons. Instead, the third generation of Kennedys is beginning to look more and more like its dynastical predecessors, the Adams family:

- Ted's son Patrick (also a congressman, from Rhode Island), pleaded guilty to driving under the influence of prescription drugs just as this book was going to print. In this incident, he nearly hit a police car, ignored officers' attempts to get him to pull over to the side of the road, and finally crashed his car into a security barrier near the U.S. Capitol.
- Robert's son David died of a drug overdose.
- Robert's son Robert Jr. was arrested for possession of heroin in 1983; he was working as an assistant district attorney at the time.
- Ted's daughter, Kara, was in and out of halfway houses in the 1970s as she fought an addiction to drugs.
- Ted's son Ted Jr. was once arrested for possession of marijuana.
- Christopher Kennedy Lawford was arrested in 1980 for attempting to impersonate a doctor so he could buy the prescription drug Darvon; later that year he was arrested again when he tried to buy some heroin.
- Robert S. Shriver was busted in the early seventies for possessing marijuana.
- Jean Kennedy Smith's son, William Kennedy Smith, became very famous very fast when he was accused of rape. He was acquitted but ran into the law again when he popped a club bouncer in the nose and was arrested for assault and battery.
- Michael Kennedy, RFK's son, died in December 1997 in a freak skiing accident, which proved to be the unfortunate end to allegations of a five-year affair with the family's nineteen-year-old babysitter.

PROPHECY!

WHO'S WHO IN THE KENNEDY CLAN?

There're just so darn many of them, it's hard to keep them straight.

Joe Sr. and Rose Kennedy had nine children: Rosemary, Joe Jr., Kathleen, JFK, Eunice, Patricia, RFK, Jean, and Ted. These nine Kennedy children, in turn, had twenty-nine kids of their own:

- JFK and Jackie Bouvier Kennedy had two kids: Caroline and John.
- Eunice Kennedy Shriver and Sargent Shriver had five children: Robert, Maria, Timothy, Mark, and Anthony.
- Patricia Kennedy Lawford and Peter Lawford had four children: Christopher, Sydney, Victoria, and Robin.
- RFK and Ethel Skatel Kennedy had eleven kids: Kathleen, Joe II, Robert Jr., David, Mary Courtney, Michael, Mary Kerry, Chris, Matthew, Douglas, and Rory.
- Jean Kennedy Smith and Stephen Smith had four children: Stephen Jr., William, Amanda, and Kym.
- Ted Kennedy and Joan Bennett Kennedy had three children: Kara, Edward Jr., and Patrick.

THE ADAMS FAMILY

THE ADAMSES WERE the first family to view the presidency as a crown or an honor to be handed down from one generation to the next. However, unlike the Kennedys, who often seemed to suffer from a rather grand view of themselves, many members of the Adams family suffered from the affliction of depression.

John Adams was the first vice president of the United States and the second president—but he didn't relate well with the public and wasn't very popular. In fact, he was the first president to run for a second term and not be reelected. (Ironically, his son John Quincy was the second president to run for reelection and be denied a second term by the voting public.)

PRESIDENT JOHN ADAMS HAD THREE SONS

- John Quincy, who became as unpopular a president as his father and suffered from manic depression
- Charles, who died the ugly and lonely death of an alcoholic in a run-down apartment in New York City
- Thomas, who also died as a result of his alcoholism

JOHN ADAMS'S SON JOHN QUINCY ALSO HAD THREE SONS

George Washington Adams, who John Quincy and his wife, Louisa, expected to become president, instead suffered from horrible anxiety attacks and paranoia (much as his father and grandfather did). An alcoholic and drug addict as well, he killed himself just after his twenty-eighth birthday.

John II was encouraged to pursue an interest in public service but was also trained to run the Adams family mills. As the mills went bankrupt under his watch, he drank more and more until he finally died at thirty-one from a variety of alcohol-related causes.

Charles Francis was also expected to go into some avenue of public service and in fact was elected to the same seat in the House of Representatives his father (John Quincy Adams) had held for seventeen years after serving as president. Charles Francis later ran for governor of Massachusetts but lost.

CHARLES FRANCIS HAD FIVE SONS
(TWO OF WHOM ARE WORTH NOTING HERE)

Son Henry was both a history professor at Harvard and a successful author. Like many others in his family, he, too, suffered from tremendous periods of depression, compounded by the fact that his wife committed suicide.

Brooks, like his brother, was also a historian and a writer and also suffered from depression. He was the last of the Adams family to die. Shortly before his death he wrote: "It is not full four generations since John Adams wrote the constitution of Massachusetts. It is time that we perished. The world is tired of us."

JOHN ADAMS: A FIRM BELIEVER IN BIG GOVERNMENT

If JOHN ADAMS had had his way, our government would have been more of a monarchy. For instance, he thought many of the positions of power in the new government should be handed down from generation to generation within families. And instead of calling our leader "President of the United States," he preferred a more robust title—something like "His Highness, the President of the United States and Protector of Their Liberties" ("His Highness" for short). How much of this was motivated by the fact he figured he was next in line for the job is not known. But it is known he and Thomas Jefferson didn't get along—while Adams was a firm believer in big government, Jefferson believed "government is best which governs least."

A Family of Bad Sports

John Adams was the first president to run for reelection and lose to his challenger. He was such a bad loser that he didn't even stick around long enough to attend his challenger's inauguration.

The second president to run for reelection and lose was John Adams's son John Quincy. Like his father, he, too, was a sore loser and left town without attending the inauguration of his opponent.

WILLIAM MCKINLEY DEMONSTRATES WHY YOU SHOULD NEVER TEMPT FATE

WILLIAM MCKINLEY ALWAYS wore a red carnation in his lapel for good luck. No matter what.

One day, in an act that was completely uncharacteristic of him, President McKinley took off his lucky flower and offered it to a little girl he spotted in the crowd surrounding him.

Moments later, an assassin shot him. Eighty days later he was dead.

THE MARTHA STEWART OF ASSASSINS

WHILE WAITING FOR a train at the B&O station in Washington, James Garfield was shot and killed by an anarchist named Charles Guiteau.

Guiteau shot Garfield in the back using a five-barrel, .44-caliber pistol called a British Bulldog. Guiteau claimed he chose the gun for a very good reason: He thought it would look really good on display in a museum someday.

Guess the joke was on Guiteau: More than a hundred years after he shot the president, no one in Washington has a clue as to where his fancy gun might be—not the Smithsonian, not the National Archive, not the FBI's weapon collection in Washington, not even the U.S. Attorney's office, which prosecuted the case.

On the other hand, other pieces of memorabilia associated with the assassination are easy to put one's finger on; for instance, the National Museum of Heath and Medicine at Walter Reed Army Medical Center in Washington D.C. has Guiteau's skeleton (but not the skull), what is left of his brain (part of it was removed for medical study), and, for some strange reason, his spleen. The museum also has three of Garfield's vertebrae that were struck by Guiteau's bullet. But, alas, Guiteau's showcase pistol is nowhere to be found.

PROPHECY!

Not!

"We in America today are nearer to the final triumph over poverty than ever before in the history of any land. The poorhouse is vanishing from among us. We have not yet reached the goal but, given a chance to go forward with the policies of the last eight years, we shall soon with the help of God be in sight of the day when poverty will be banished from this nation."

—Herbert Hoover, upon accepting the Republican nomination for president in 1928. Less than a year later the stock market crashed and the nation was plunged into the darkness of the Great Depression.

Poor, Poor Herbert Hoover

The guy was so desperate to end the Depression he began grasping at straws for a solution, no matter how ridiculous. Case in point: He offered pop singer Rudy Vallee a medal if only the singer would "sing a song that would make people forget their troubles and the Depression."

WALK SOFTLY AND CARRY
A BIG SUPERSTITION

- Woodrow Wilson was superstitious about the number thirteen—there were thirteen letters in his name and thirteen original colonies when the United States was founded—and he believed it was his lucky number. Therefore, when once sailing from the United States to Europe for a peace conference, he made sure the ship slowed down so he wouldn't arrive on the twelfth but on the thirteenth instead.

- Neither FDR and his family nor Herbert Hoover and his family would ever sit at a table set for thirteen guests. Additionally, FDR refused to travel on a Friday and would never allow himself to be third on a single match. (This last one was a common superstition among smokers, believe by some to have originated in World War I. The idea was that it was unlucky to be the third person to light his cigar or cigarette from one match. Why? Because in wartime, the striking of the match might get a sniper's attention, allowing him to take aim while the second soldier lit up and then pick off the unlucky third soldier.)

- Ronald Reagan believed knocking on wood brings good luck.

- Warren Harding, a career newspaper man, always carried a printer's rule in his vest pocket for good luck.

- Ulysses S. Grant had a thing about retracing his footsteps; anytime he inadvertantly passed his intended destination, he would never turn around and go back exactly the way he came but would take another route, even if it meant he would have to travel far out of his way. You might think this was a charming little neurosis—unless you were on a battlefield under General Grant's command and it was time to retreat.

8

Death!

"Boys, if you ever pray, pray for me now."

—One of Harry Truman's first statements
to the press after being sworn in as president
following the death of FDR

"HELLO . . . MR. PRESIDENT?"

Ever wonder what goes on behind the scenes when the president dies? Here's how James David Barber, in his book *Presidential Character,* reported on the transfer of presidential power to Harry Truman following FDR's death:

> The President's death caught [Vice President] Truman entirely by surprise. On April 11, 1945, Harry was his usual ebullient self. When the Senate adjourned that day the reporters flocked around him; one called him "Mr. President," as Senators address their presiding officer. Truman flashed a smile and said, "Boys, those are fighting words out in Missouri where I come from. You'd better smile when you say that! . . ."
>
> The next day he whiled away the afternoon on the rostrum writing a newsy letter home, telling his folks to be sure to tune in when, tomorrow night, he would make a speech and introduce the President. At 5:10 he strolled over to Sam Rayburn's "Board of Education" hideaway in the House end of the Capitol where Rayburn's friends often gathered at the end of the day to open a bottle and "strike a blow for liberty." Rayburn gave him the message to call the White House immediately. "Please come right over," he was told, "and come in through the main Pennsylvania entrance."
>
> His face turned white. "Holy General Jackson!" he said, raced back to his office, found his chauffeur, and made it to the White House at 5:25, where he was immediately directed to Mrs. Roosevelt's study.
>
> "Harry," Eleanor said, "the President is dead."
>
> Truman was stunned into silence. Finally he choked out, "Is there anything I can do for you?"
>
> Eleanor replied, "Is there anything we can do for you? For you are the one in trouble now."
>
> The next day, Truman's first as president, was Friday the thirteenth of April.

"SO HELP ME GOD"

IN HIS BOOK *Madmen and Geniuses,* Sol Barzman sets the stage for the death of Warren G. Harding and the swearing in of Calvin Coolidge:

> In late July he [Harding] suffered a collapse in Seattle and was moved to San Francisco, where he died in a few days, apparently of a heart attack. The date was August 2, 1923; Harding was fifty-five.
>
> The vice president, in the meantime, had taken his family to his birthplace in Plymouth Notch, Vermont, for a summer vacation. They were staying at his father's farmhouse, which had neither electricity nor a telephone.
>
> It was not until midnight, when the Coolidges had already been asleep for some hours, that an excited messenger came chugging up in an ancient automobile with the news that the president was dead. While oil lamps were lit, and reporters and neighbors gathered, the vice president calmly dressed in a dark suit, came downstairs, and prepared to take the oath of office as the thirtieth president of the United States.
>
> In a room with faded wallpaper, a threadbare rug, and an oil lamp for illumination, the elderly Coolidge, who was a notary public, became the first and only father ever to swear in his own son as president.
>
> When the last phrase of the oath was spoken, the new president solemnly placed his hand on the Bible and spoke the final words with fitting sincerity:
>
> "So help me God."
>
> A few minutes later, he returned upstairs, went back to bed, and fell asleep almost at once.

It's interesting to note that Harding was soon to be up for reelection, and he had no intention of asking Calvin Coolidge to run again as his running mate.

DEATH!

"WHO'S IN CHARGE HERE?"

ACCORDING TO ARTICLE II, Section I of the Constitution, when the president is no longer able to serve, the vice president shall inherit his job.

But should he?

This particular passage of the Constitution reads:

> In Case of Removal of the President from Office, or of his Death, Resignation, or Inability to discharge the Powers and Duties of the said Office, the Same shall devolve on the Vice President.

John Tyler was the first vice president to gain the office of the presidency as a result of the death of the president when William Henry Harrison died a month after taking office. Unfortunately for Tyler, this also meant it was the first time the above passage of the Constitution was put to the test.

While some agreed with Tyler's interpretation—that he should automatically assume the job of president—others (like John Quincy Adams) argued that the vice president should gain the "Powers and Duties" of the office but not the office itself.

The difference?

Tyler insisted he should become president, while his detractors insisted that he merely fulfill the duties of president without receiving the title. The problem arose over the wording of the Constitution, with Tyler interpreting the word *Same* to apply to the "same Office" while his detractors argued that *Same* referred only to the president's "Powers and Duties."

This controversy led to some

At least he didn't call it "Whitewater."

While president, Tyler bought an estate in Charles City County, Virginia, called "Creek Plantation." He changed the name of the estate to "Sherwood Forest" because, as he explained, he felt like a political outlaw.

interesting situations—one of which may have inspired the movie *Miracle on 34th Street*. Just as in the movie Santa's existence is proven by the ability of the postal service to deliver mail to him, whenever mail was sent to the White House addressed to "Acting President" or some variation of that theme, Tyler would return it unopened.

Just don't accuse him of being a White House intern.

Rumor has it that when a messenger arrived at Tyler's house to tell him President Harrison had died, he was on his hands and knees on the floor playing marbles.

Tyler's detractors were many, for he was elected to the position of vice president as a Whig, inherited the presidency a month after taking office, and then so outraged the Whig Party with his policies that they actually kicked him out of the party—while he was still president!

Furthermore, those who disagreed with Tyler's interpretation of the Constitution on the issue of the vice president's succession to the presidency were sufficiently outraged with him to begin taking steps to rectify the situation. Thus Tyler became not only the first vice president to succeed to the presidency but also the first to face possible impeachment. (The drive for impeachment didn't have enough supporters in Congress, however, and no resolution to begin impeachment proceedings was ever passed.) As if all this wasn't enough, as the sitting president Tyler suffered the ultimate humiliation of receiving no presidential nomination from either party in the election of 1844.

This vein of controversy followed Tyler to his grave. When he died there was no official recognition of his death or his service to his country by the federal government, a sharp contrast to how the government had treated the deaths of other former presidents. Although Tyler died in 1862, it wasn't until 1911 that the federal government recognized his service by appropriating ten thousand dollars for the building of a memorial in his name. At the dedication of that memorial in 1915, only five senators and five members of the House of Representatives were in attendance.

DEATH!

"Here lies the body of my good horse 'The General.' For twenty years he bore me around the circuit of my practice and in all that time he never made a blunder. Would that his master could say the same."

—The inscription on John Tyler's horse's grave

"I'M IN CHARGE NOW!"

—Secretary of State Alexander Haig, incorrectly
assuming power of the United States government
just moments after Ronald Reagan was shot

So LET'S GET this straight for General Haig and anyone else who is confused over who succeeds the president should he die or become unable to fulfill the duties of his job.

IF THE PRESIDENT DIES

The following order dictates who will serve as acting president until the end of the current term:

1. Vice president
2. Speaker of the House
3. President pro tempore of the Senate
4. Secretary of state
5. Secretary of the treasury
6. Secretary of defense
7. Attorney general
8. Secretary of the interior
9. Secretary of agriculture
10. Secretary of commerce
11. Secretary of labor
12. Secretary of health and human services

AND IF THE PRESIDENT IS DISABLED . . .

The vice president acts as president but does not assume the job itself.

The president can declare himself disabled and request that the vice president assume his duties. Additionally, the president can be declared disabled (should the president be unconscious, for instance) by a majority vote of the vice president and the members of the president's cabinet. In either case, it is the president's right to determine when he is able to assume the powers and duties of the office again.

If the vice president and members of the cabinet disagree with the president's assessment of his own fitness, they can request that both Houses of Congress put the matter to a vote. A two-thirds vote is required by both Houses to overrule the president's wish to return to power.

ACTUALLY, GENERAL HAIG, YOU'VE GOT IT WRONG. THE PRESIDENT'S STILL IN CHARGE.

"I hope you're all Republicans."

—Reagan's quip to the surgeons who were about
to operate on him after he was shot

I<small>T'S WORTH MENTIONING</small> that Reagan kept a much cooler head after being shot than did his secretary of state Alexander Haig—while the general was putting his foot in his mouth, the wounded president was entertaining the troops with a string of one-liners.

"Honey, I forgot to duck!" was the first thing Reagan said to his wife, Nancy, after he was shot. What an actor! Is it possible he remembered, even under those circumstances, that this was the same thing boxer Jack Dempsey had said to his wife fifty-five years earlier after he was pulverized in the ring by Gene Tunney?

PRESIDENT . . . FOR A DAY

ONLY ONCE HAS the country been under the leadership of someone other than the president or vice president.

Sort of.

It happened on March 4, 1849, when Inauguration Day fell on a Sunday and president-elect Zachary Taylor refused to be inaugurated on the Sabbath. This created a bit of a stir because, even though he refused to take his vow of office that day, the law still said that on March 4 at noon the current president and vice president would cease to be in power.

What to do? Well, according to the laws at the time, and if the position of vice president were ever vacant, it would be filled immediately by the president pro tem of the Senate. (If the position of president were ever vacant, it would be filled immediately by the vice president.) For all the reasons stated above, at noon on Sunday, March 4, 1849, the current president, James Polk, and his vice president, George Dallas, completed their terms in office, and David Rice Atchinson, president pro tem of the Senate, became vice president. And at twelve o'clock on the same day, acting Vice President David Rice Atchinson also stepped in to become president of the United States.

"NOPE. YOU'RE NOT INVITED."

Every year, when the president delivers his State of the Union address, there is one member of his cabinet who is not invited.

Think about it: The president's got to be there, obviously. And the vice president's got to be there to show his support for his boss. And the prez, of course, wants the rest of his cabinet there to cheer him on. . . .

But what if something happened? A devastating earthquake or a terrorist attack or a bomb? What if everyone in the room were killed? Who would lead the nation?

By law, therefore, at least one member of the president's cabinet is required to stay away on the night of the State of the Union address in case such a disaster occurs.

HOW TO BEAT AN ASSASSIN AT HIS OWN GAME

It wasn't until 1901, when William McKinley was assassinated, that the president began receiving protection. Yet the first president to have an attempt made on his life was Andrew Jackson.

His would-be assassin was Richard Lawrence, a house painter who thought the president was the only thing standing between him and the British throne. Lawrence actually shot at the president twice, using two different guns.

But go figure the odds of this: Both guns misfired—an event that statisticians say could only occur once in 125,000 tries.

Once Jackson got over the shock of being shot at, he chased after Lawrence with his walking stick.

DEATH!

"QUICK! CALL A LAWYER!"
PRESIDENT DIES OF MALPRACTICE

James Garfield didn't die from gunshot wounds—he died of blood poisoning after doctors tried to fish a bullet out of his back with their dirty fingers and instruments. (Poor guy. He took the bullet in the back before doctors had a clue about infections, so they didn't even bother washing their hands before they started poking around in his wound.)

If Garfield showed up at an emergency room today with the same wounds, the doctors in attendance probably would have left the bullet right where it was. And then they would have sent him home after a few days of observation and bed rest—instead of causing him to linger on in pain for eighty days before dying.

In fact, during his trial Garfield's assassin, Charles Guiteau, claimed he wasn't the one that killed the president; that job, he claimed, had been done by his doctors.

{ "Go out and buy every pound of ice you can find! Hurry! This stifling air is killing the president!" }

—First Lady Lucretia Garfield

Unbeknownst to most, the shooting of President Garfield provided the catalyst for the invention of the first air conditioner.

First, he was surrounded by blocks of ice while his wife and staffers waved fans to blow the cooler air over his body—but this had only the slightest impact on the heat.

Next, an inventor named R. S. Jennings and a group of military engineers tried to build a cooling system using ice water and an electric fan—which brought the temperature of the room down but made it so humid it was almost impossible to breathe.

Finally, after seventy-two hours of nonstop work, a system was developed that pumped cool air from three tons of ice into the president's room while the moisture from the melting ice was channeled away via a series of Rube Goldberg-like tubes and ducts.

Air conditioning was born. But eighty days after he was shot, the president died. When it comes to the medical sciences, it's amazing what a difference thirty years makes:

- Garfield was shot in 1881.
- Doctors tried to remove Garfield's bullet.
- Garfield died eighty days after he was shot.

- Teddy Roosevelt was shot in 1912.
- Doctors left Roosevelt's bullet right where it landed.
- Roosevelt lived for seven more years.

AND TO ADD INSULT TO INJURY

If his doctors had found the bullet, President Garfield might have had a good chance of living. However, since the doctors couldn't find it they just kept poking around with their dirty hands and medical tools, thus making matters worse.

Interestingly, one method they used to try to find the bullet involved a brand-new invention by Alexander Graham Bell: a metal detector. And it might have helped too—if Garfield hadn't been lying on a metal bed!

"I AM GOING TO ASK YOU TO BE VERY QUIET. IF YOU'LL DO THAT, I WILL DO THE BEST I CAN."

—Teddy Roosevelt
(How else do you begin a speech when the audience knows you've just been shot in the chest? Roosevelt talked for eighty minutes—then agreed to go to the hospital to be examined.)

During Teddy Roosevelt's second run for the presidency he became the first former president to survive an assassination attempt.

He was shot while in Milwaukee to deliver a speech, and still delivered the speech with the bullet in his chest. Afterward, he was rushed to a hospital, where it was discovered that the bullet had nicked his glasses case, slowing its impact. Additionally, Roosevelt had written his speech by hand on single pieces of paper in large letters with wide spaces for easy reading, so the fifty-page speech (which he had folded in half and put in his left breast pocket) helped slow the speed of the bullet.

"No doubt about it," commented Roosevelt's doctor, Alexander Lamber, "His speech saved his life."

{ "I don't mind it any more than if it were in my waistcoat pocket." }

—TR, making an observation about the bullet in his chest many years after he was shot

Dead Dumb

On July 4, 1850, in the fourth year of his presidency, Zachary Taylor attended a ceremony for the laying of the corner-stone of the Washington Monument. While at the reception, he ate a huge amount of cold cherries and pickled cucumbers and drank a massive quantity of iced milk. Five days later he was dead of gastroenteritis.

James Polk worked so hard at being president that he may have worked himself to death. For the full four years of his presidency, he worked twelve to fourteen hours a day; he hated to stop working even to eat. Three months after he left office, he was dead of exhaustion.

DEATH!

DEAD DOG

WARREN HARDING LOVED dogs.

In fact, he loved his own dog, Laddie Boy, so much that he arranged for him to be assigned Dog License #1 and threw him a birthday party at the White House, where he was served a cake made of layered dog biscuits covered with frosting.

Another time, Harding heard about a dog that had been brought into the country illegally and was going to be put to death by the order of a Pennsylvania judge. Harding was so moved by the story he wrote a letter to the governor of Pennsylvania requesting a pardon for the dog . . . which the governor granted.

When the newspaperman-turned-politician died, the Newsboys Association of America, of which Harding was also president, decided to build a statue of Laddie Boy as a tribute to him. To raise money for the statue, the newsboys association asked each newspaper boy in America to donate a penny. One hundred and three pounds of pennies were collected and then melted down to provide the bronze for the statue.

The statue of Laddie Boy can still be seen today at the Smithsonian Institution.

DEATH DEFYING

Health. Fitness. It's a national craze.

Here are a few odd things presidents have done to maintain their health, ward off illness, or otherwise tempt the hands of fate:

- Ronald and Nancy Reagan gave up smoking after their good friend Robert Taylor died of lung cancer. As the story goes, Reagan needed something to help him kick the habit, and his love of jellybeans was born.
- Thomas Jefferson was convinced that if he soaked his feet in a bucket of cold water every day, he'd never get a cold.
- Sure to cure what ails ya': Calvin Coolidge used to like having his head rubbed with petroleum jelly while he ate his breakfast in bed.
- After Woodrow Wilson's first wife died, his doctor encouraged him to take up the game of golf to help him relax and get over her death. Wilson fell in love with the game and was soon playing every day before breakfast. He liked playing so much, in fact, that in winter he would paint his golf balls black so he could continue playing in the snow.
- Ulysses S. Grant had a pack-a-day habit—only it wasn't twenty cigarettes he smoked every day, it was twenty cigars.

> "Since I came to the White House, I got two hearing aids, a colon operation, skin cancer, a prostate operation, and I was shot. The damn thing is I've never felt better in my life."
> —Ronald Reagan in 1987

DEATH!

Finally . . .
the answer is here!

Q: Who is buried in Grant's Tomb?

A: No one. No one is *ever* buried in a tomb—tombs are always above ground.

- No one liked a good toothpick more than Warren G. Harding. In fact, he had the White House staff stash them all around the house so he would never have to travel far to get one.
- Jimmy Carter had problems with his stomach and feet that made him think he'd never get into the navy. To cure his flat feet he would stand around on Coke bottles (being from Georgia, Pepsi just wouldn't do) and roll them back and forth under his feet. The problem with his stomach was even more easily solved: He carried a bucket around the ship with him when it was his turn to stand watch.

"PSSSSSST! CATO, IS THAT YOU?"

Much like Inspector Clouseau of the Pink Panther movies, Teddy Roosevelt lived for his violent and relentless daily exercise. He fought with Japanese jujitsu experts and Chinese wrestlers in the East Room. He walked hard, running his friends down and challenging the Secret Service men who were there to protect him to keep up as he crossed rivers and streams, climbed up and down hills, and cut through the underbrush. He played tennis and rode horseback daily. He was also the first president to jog; he ran around the Washington Monument every day.

Once, while boxing with a young naval officer, he took a blow to the left eye that eventually caused him to lose the use of it (although Teddy kept this a secret for many years so the naval officer wouldn't feel guilty).

> { "I do little boxing now because it seems rather absurd for a president to appear with a black eye or a swollen nose or a cut lip." }
>
> —Teddy Roosevelt

DEATH!

THIS KIND OF TALK CAN KILL YOU

THE RECORD FOR both the longest inauguration speech and the shortest presidency both belong to one man: William Henry Harrison. Harrison died after only thirty-one days in office, and it's fair to say that he talked himself into his grave.

Here's the longer version of the story:

Harrison's inauguration was on a cold and wet day, yet Harrison refused to wear a hat, coat, or gloves and insisted on participating in all of the outdoor events. This included the presentation of his inauguration speech, which was 8,578 words long and lasted one hour and forty-five minutes.

One month later Harrison was dead from pneumonia.

"Excuse me? Did you say something?"

It was George Washington who made the shortest inauguration speech on record—133 words and less than two minutes long.

MODEST TO THE END

BEFORE HE DIED Thomas Jefferson wrote his own epitaph:

> Here was buried Thomas Jefferson, author of the Declaration of Independence, of the Statuette of Virginia for Religious Freedom, and the father of the University of Virginia.

You'll notice Jefferson neglected to mention he had ever been the president of the United States.

CURSES!

WHEN WILLIAM HENRY Harrison was a young man fighting at the Battle of Tippercanoe, a Shawnee Indian put a curse on his head. As a result, they say, Harrison died a month after he took office. And until 1980 all other presidents elected in a year ending in zero also died while in office—Lincoln, McKinley, Harding, Kennedy.

DEATH!

MORE CURSES!

CALL IT CHARACTER assassination if you want. Or call it death of a career.

When the leader of Haiti, Jean Claude Duvalier, came to the conclusion that Jimmy Carter was treating him and his countrymen badly, he did the only logical thing: He headed for the backyard at midnight on a dark Haitian night and put a curse on the president's head by chanting and throwing a live bull, some photos of Carter, and a lot of dirt into a very large hole.

Did it work? You be the judge. Shortly after Duvalier cast his midnight spell:

- Fifty-two American hostages were taken in Iran during an election year and Carter couldn't get them out.

- Inflation soared out of control, and prime interest rates reached as high as 20 percent.

- Carter's popularity plunged.

- Carter lost the 1980 election to Ronald Reagan.

DEATH WISH

- According to family history, George Washington insisted he be embalmed in whiskey for three days after his death, just to be sure he was really gone before they buried him.

- Andrew Jackson, who came within one Senate vote of being impeached, requested he be buried with a copy of the Constitution under his head as a pillow and the Stars and Stripes wrapped over him like a shroud.

- One might have thought "Silent Cal" Coolidge would use his will as the instrument to finally speak his mind, but he didn't. Instead he left this world in the same spirit in which he had lived—practically silent. Coolidge's entire will, in which he left everything he owned to his wife and made it quite explicit he was leaving nothing to his one surviving son, consisted of one sentence.

- JFK, who was independently wealthy and a member of one of the richest and most powerful families in the country, left his wife all of his "personal effects, furniture, furnishings, silverware, dishes, china, glassware, and linens, which I may own at the time of death" along with a grand total of twenty-five thousand dollars in cash.

- When Andrew Johnson died, his family wanted to "do the right thing" and throw him a proper funeral. But before Johnson died he had expressly forbade them to call in a minister to do the job.

> "Please put
> out the light."
>
> —Teddy Roosevelt's last
> request before dying

DEATH!

> "This is the fourth?"
>
> —Thomas Jefferson's last words; the first time he asked, it was still July 3

DEAD LAST

EVER WONDER JUST how far you could take a rivalry?

While John Adams lay dying on July 4, 1826—exactly fifty years to the day after the Declaration of Independence was signed—he resigned himself to the fact that his most bitter political rival, Thomas Jefferson, would live on and beat him again.

Thus Adams's last words were, "Thomas Jefferson survives."

Little did Adams know that Jefferson had died just a few hours earlier.

9

Goofballs!

WELL, MAYBE IF people tiptoed around you all the time and were always calling you "the most powerful man in the world," you might start to believe it too. And all that power might start to affect your behavior in some pretty strange ways.

On the other hand, if you're like us, you've probably already done some pretty strange things, never once imagining that every small utterance and tiny goofy act you ever committed would someday be scrutinized by voters, journalists, historians, and nosy busybodies like you and us.

Such is the lot of the president: Every moment of his life is under a microscope, even those years before he even entertained the notion that he would someday become president.

GOOFBALL-AT-A-GLANCE

President: **George Washington**

Random goofy act: Washington didn't have enough money to get to his own inauguration, so he had to borrow six hundred dollars from a neighbor. ◄━ ━ ━┓

Or maybe he just couldn't find an ATM?

President: **John Adams**

Random goofy acts: While he was serving as the U.S. minister to England and Thomas Jefferson was serving as the U.S. minister to France, the two men made a trip to Stratford-upon-Avon to visit the birthplace of William Shakespeare. While there, they took a knife to one of Shakespeare's chairs so they could take home some woodchips as souvenirs.

He and his wife once got lost in the woods of Washington D.C. on their way to the White House. They might still be there if a passing stranger hadn't shown them the way home.

President: **Thomas Jefferson**

Random goofy acts: He had the honor of leading the first inaugural parade through Washington. However, a parade wasn't exactly what he had in mind—he was just walking back to his boarding house after being sworn in, and a bunch of people decided to follow.

When the British minister to the United States arrived at the White House for his first meeting with the new president, Jefferson received him wearing only his robe and slippers.

President:	**James Madison**
Random goofy act:	He and Thomas Jefferson were once arrested together for taking a carriage ride in the countryside of Vermont on a Sunday, which violated the blue laws of that state.

President:	**James Monroe**
Random goofy act:	Poor James Monroe . . . when it was time for him to be inaugurated, he couldn't have his ceremony in the chamber of the House of Representatives as all his predecessors had done. The problem? He and Speaker of the House Henry Clay were having a tiff, so Clay put his foot down and refused to let Monroe use the hall.

- → America's first cover-up in the press!

President:	**John Quincy Adams**
Random goofy acts:	While president, he would often go from the White House to the edge of the Potomac River, shuck off his clothes, throw them on a rock, and go skinny-dipping. One day, when he returned to the rock, he found a reporter sitting on his mound of clothes. And it wasn't just any reporter. It was a woman named Anne Royal. And she refused to leave until the president granted her an interview. Adams was only too happy to oblige her request—without getting out of the river, of course.

There is an additional irony to this story: There was Royal sitting on his clothes, yet when John Quincy was back at the White House he did not like "regular" people to sit in his presence, so he would make sure there weren't enough chairs to go around.

GOOFBALLS!

President:	**Andrew Jackson**
Random goofy acts:	One of the first things he did after being elected president was to order twenty spittoons for the White House parlors.
	He was the first president to be handed a baby to kiss as a part of his campaigning duties—but he declined the offer and passed the baby to his secretary of war instead.
	When he sent his first annual message to Congress in 1829, it was so well received that no one could believe he wrote it. When he was accused point-blank of having sent in a message written by someone else, he replied, "Don't I deserve just as much credit for picking out the man who could write it?"
	While president, he kept a stable of thoroughbreds on the White House grounds. But when he entered them into races at a nearby track, he used an alias so no one would know they were his.

Can you guess what came between him and his Calvin Kleins?

President:	**Martin Van Buren**
Random goofy act:	Rumor has it he was quite a dandy and used to dab a little cologne on his whiskers and lace himself up in a corset every day.

President:	**William Henry Harrison**
Random goofy acts:	His campaign slogan during the 1840 presidential campaign was "Keep the Ball Rolling to Washington." Of course his supporters had no choice but to roll a huge ball of paper across the country to the Whig convention in Baltimore.

Harrison was sometimes called "General Mum" because he never spoke out on any of the major issues while campaigning for president. This was no accident; the truth was that he had nothing to say.

"Wunnerful! Wunnerful!"

President:	**John Tyler**
Random goofy act:	He loved to dance. In fact, he's the guy who made the polka an American household word.

President:	**James Polk**
Random goofy acts:	At age sixteen he had an operation to have his gallstones removed . . . and demanded the operation be done without anesthesia.

A matter of great concern to him as president was how to protect his arm from injury after a day of handshaking . . . and he was sure he'd found the trick:

> I could shake hands during the whole day without suffering any bad effects from it. . . . If a man surrendered his arm to be shaken, by some horizontally, by others perpendicularly, and by others again with a strong grip, he could not fail to suffer severely from it, but that if he would shake and not be shaken, grip and not be gripped, taking care always to

GOOFBALLS!

squeeze the hand of his adversary as hard as he squeezed him, that he suffered no inconvenience from it. . . . I could generally anticipate when I was to have a strong grip, and that when I observed a strong man approaching I generally took advantage of him by being a little quicker then he was and seizing him by the tips of his fingers, giving him a hearty shake, and thus preventing him from getting a full grip upon me.

Maybe Polk Wasn't So Goofy After All

In the good old days when security was less of a problem and there were events at the White House that were open to the public, presidents would sometimes shake as many as eight thousand hands at a stretch, at the rate of forty to fifty per minute. On one particular occasion, after Abe Lincoln had spent a full three hours at a reception pressing the flesh before signing an important bill, he found his arm was "almost paralyzed" and it was next to impossible for him to hold onto a pen. After dropping his writing instrument once, he persevered and picked it up again . . . to sign the Emancipation Proclamation into law.

President:	**Zachary Taylor**
Random goofy act:	He had no political experience when nominated for president, had never voted before, and didn't even know what party he belonged to. When the notification of his nomination for president arrived in the mail, he didn't respond to it—not because he didn't want the job but because he was too cheap to pay the ten cents of postage due.

President:	**Millard Fillmore**
Random goofy acts:	One of his greatest accomplishments as president? He successfully negotiated a treaty with Peru for the use of bird droppings.

Another of Fillmore's great accomplishments? He bought the White House's first stove. When the cook couldn't figure out how to use it, Fillmore went down to the Patent Office, studied the drawings until he understood how it worked, then went back to the White House and taught the cook.

207

President:	**Franklin Pierce**
Random goofy act:	"Ben, they tell me you are going to vote for the abolition resolutions. Now, I am not here, of course, to dictate to you; but if you vote for those resolutions . . . you are no brother of mine; I will never speak to you again."

GOOFBALLS!

Just Like Motel 6, Part One:
The highest-priced rooms of any national chain

President:	**James Buchanan**
Random goofy act:	James Buchanan was the first president to be visited by a member of the Royal Family. Buchanan considered the visit to be such an honor that he let Prince Albert Edward sleep in his bed while he slept on a couch out in the hall.

President:	**Abraham Lincoln**
Random goofy acts:	It was during a cabinet meeting at which all his cabinet members disagreed with him that he summed up his position this way: "Seven nays, one aye; the ayes have it."

Once, before he was president, he led twenty or so soldiers on a march during the Black Hawk Indian War. When they reached a fence with a gate, he couldn't for the life of him remember the proper marching order to give the men so they would proceed single file through the gate. So, after thinking for a minute, he ordered, "This company is dismissed for two minutes, when it will fall in again on the other side of the gate."

He is the only president to have faced enemy fire while in office. It happened when he was visiting Fort Stevens during the Civil War; he mounted a parapet to get a better view of the battlefield, and being six feet four, he made an easy mark. Rumor has it that when a solider (said to be future Supreme Court Justice Oliver Wendell Holmes) shouted at him to "Get down, you damned fool, before you get shot!" the president did as he was told.

No one loved puns and wordplay more than he did. When Stephen Douglas referred to him as "two-faced," he replied by asking, "If I had another face, do you think I would wear this one?" When he saw a heavyset woman in a large feathered cap fall down as she was crossing the street, he commented: "Reminds me of a duck. . . . She's got feathers on her head and down on her behind." And when he heard a rumor that Edward Stanton, his secretary of war, had called him "a damned fool," he gave this honest reply: "If Stanton said I was a damned fool, then I must be one, for he is nearly always right and generally says what he means."

President:	**Andrew Johnson**
Random goofy acts:	Before he got into politics, he was a tailor—the only tailor ever to be elected president. Even as president it was rare for him to pass a tailor shop—no matter where he was—without stopping in to say hello. He was so proud of his skill with a needle and thread that while governor of Tennessee he took time out from his gubernatorial duties to make a suit for a friend, who just happened to be the governor of Kentucky. The grateful governor, previously a blacksmith, sent him a shovel and a pair of tongs in return.

Even as president, Johnson wore only suits that were tailor-made . . . by his own hand.

| Random goofy acts: | As a boy, his father sent him to a neighbor's house to buy a colt for which his father had already offered twenty dollars but that the neighbor insisted was worth twenty-five. The last set of instructions his father gave him was to offer twenty, and if the neighbor wouldn't take it, to offer twenty-two-fifty. Only as a last resort was he to offer the full twenty-five. When he got to the neighbor's house he immediately reported: "Papa says I may offer you twenty dollars for the colt, but if you won't take that I am to offer twenty-two and a half, and if you won't take that, to give you twenty-five." |

He was actually given the name Hiram Ulysses Grant but hated the acronym his name created: HUG. Therefore, when his name was incorrectly recorded as Ulysses Simpson Grant while a student at West Point, he never bothered to point out the error.

210

Although a great war hero, anytime Grant saw blood or a piece of raw meat, his head would start to spin.

He had a thing about nudity; he didn't like it. He refused to ever get completely naked—not even to bathe—and at the age of sixty claimed that no one had seen him without clothes since he was a little boy.

While walking in the rain to a reception in his honor one day, he offered to share his umbrella with another man headed the same way. The man, it turned out, was also going to the reception and confided, "I merely go to satisfy a personal curiosity. Between us, I have always thought that Grant was very much an overrated man." "That's my view also," was Grant's reply.

Just Like Motel 6, Part Two: "Children sleep for free!"

President:	**Rutherford B. Hayes**
Random goofy act:	Like President Bill Clinton, he and his family liked to entertain a lot of guests at the White House. Sometimes, when they invited too many people to spend the night, son Webb had to sleep on top of an old billiards table in the White House attic.
President:	**James Garfield**
Random goofy act:	He was the first president to ever talk on a telephone. Here's what he said to Alexander Graham Bell, who was at the other end of a thirteen-mile wire, to mark this momentous occasion: "Please speak a little more slowly."

Bet Motel 6 wouldn't turn them away.

President:	**Chester Alan Arthur**
Random goofy act:	He enacted the country's first major immigration law: His goal was to prevent criminals, paupers, idiots, and the insane from entering the country.
President:	**Grover Cleveland**
Random goofy act:	He is the only president ever to get married in the White House. He wrote the invitations himself and worked in his office until 7 p.m. on the day of the wedding, then knocked off so he could get ready for the ceremony and reception. And while he did promise to "love, honor, and comfort" his bride, he refused to promise to "obey" her.

GOOFBALLS!

President:	Benjamin Harrison
Random goofy act:	He and his family were the first to have electricity in the White House— but they left the lights on all night because they were afraid to touch the switches.

President:	William McKinley
Random goofy act:	He loved a good cigar but wouldn't be photographed with one in his mouth; he didn't want to set a bad example for America's children, after all.

President:	Teddy Roosevelt
Random goofy acts:	While hunting one day, he came across a small bear cub and of course refused to shoot it. The incident was reported in the news, which inspired a political cartoonist to draw his interpretation of the scene, which then inspired a toy manufacturer to come out with a line of stuffed animals he called "Teddy Bears." Ironically, President Roosevelt hated to be called Teddy.
	Teddy Roosevelt . . . Madison Avenue copywriter? Well, it has been said that after drinking a cup of Maxwell House coffee while visiting Andrew Jackson's home, the Hermitage, near Nashville, Roosevelt said, "Delicious. This coffee is good to the last drop!"

President:	**William Howard Taft**
Random goofy acts:	While a young lawyer, he visited another town on business and discovered the next train home was many hours away. Taking a second look at the train schedule, he saw that a faster train would be passing soon but wasn't scheduled to stop at his station. Without hesitation he sent a wire to the superintendent of the line asking if the train could stop at his station for a large party. Of course, when he climbed aboard the train alone, the conductor looked puzzled. Taft looked him in the eye, made a gesture toward his three-hundred-pound frame, and told the conductor he was the "large party" for which the train was making the special stop.

When you're as heavy as Taft was, people will nag you to death trying to get you to lose weight. This is true even if you are president, as he found out; between his wife and his doctor, he was often on a diet, and whenever he was dieting he would get cranky. Once, when he went off on a train trip, he became enraged at discovering his wife had had the dining car removed. "What's the use of being president if you can't have a train with a diner on it?" he asked and demanded that the crew stop at the next station and restore the dining car to its rightful place.

Perhaps it was because of his size, but he sometimes had a heck of a time staying awake. His aide, Archie Butts, had one method of waking him when others were around: He would cough. His wife employed a slightly different technique: She'd give him an elbow in the ribs.

Who *is* this clown? ←---

President:	**Woodrow Wilson**
Random goofy act:	He was the first president to earn a Ph.D., but in his heart he wanted to be a vaudeville actor. As a young boy, he even ran away to join the circus—and went home with padding in his pants in anticipation of the greeting he was going to get from his father.

GOOFBALLS!

President:	**Warren Harding**
Random goofy act:	See the GOOFBALL HALL OF FAME on page 223.

President:	**Calvin Coolidge**
Random goofy act:	See VICE-GOOFBALL on page 227.

Just like Motel 6, Part Four: "Friendly Service!"

President:	**Herbert Hoover**
Random goofy act:	Under his reign the White House servants quickly learned one thing: The president didn't like to see them. According to one account:

> [Hoover] did not like seeing the servants in the halls; and so they hid when the White House bells announced his presence, footmen holding trays high in the air as they scurried into hall closets already crowded with maids.

President:	**Franklin Delano Roosevelt**
Random goofy acts:	He was a rich, good-looking guy who just happened to have a cousin in the White House. No surprise, then, that his own local politicians began to court him and encourage him to enter local politics. One story has it that when he was first approached by a local political boss and encouraged to enter the race for the New York state assembly, his first response was that he would consider it, but he wanted to talk to his mother about it first. "Frank," the local politician replied, "there are men back in Poughkeepsie waiting for your answer. They won't like to hear that you had to ask your mother."

When visited at the White House by the king and queen of England, he let Eleanor serve them hot dogs for dinner.

214

His idea of a good time was to play poker with lots of wild cards. He also loved collecting stamps and never left on a trip without taking at least one of his stamp albums with him.

He had "Stolen from the White House" embossed on the White House matches.

President:	**Harry Truman**
Random goofy acts:	He loved to use the word *manure*. Once asked why she let him use such language, his wife, Bess, explained that it took her twenty years to get him to say just that.

In his early days of politics, he joined the Ku Klux Klan in Jackson County, Missouri, because he knew he couldn't win the judge's seat he was running for without their support; a year after he was elected, he resigned his membership and got his ten-dollar membership fee back.

When he visited Disneyland he refused to ride on the "Dumbo, the Elephant" ride because he was a Democrat and the elephant, of course, is the mascot of the Republican Party.

"General Picasso, Sir!"

President:	**Dwight D. Eisenhower**
Random goofy act:	He loved to paint but couldn't draw worth a darn, so he would have someone else sketch pictures, and then he would paint inside the lines. Believe it or not, this is how the national paint-by-numbers fad of the 1950s began.

President:	**John F. Kennedy**
Random goofy acts:	As a young man, he seemed to have a good mind for his studies but was clueless about the world. As he once described himself: "Though I may not be able to remember material things such as tickets, gloves, and so on, I can remember things like *Ivanhoe*, and the last time we had an exam on it I got ninety-eight." At the age of thirteen in 1930, while the rest of the country was suffering from the debilitating effects of the stock market crash and the Great Depression, Jack wrote home: "Please send me the *Literary Digest* because I didn't know about the Market Slump until a long time after."

He had a hard time with the concept of money for all of his adult life. For one thing, he never seemed to have any cash on him—which meant his friends were constantly shelling out money to cover the costs of his cabs and dinners and movies. Perhaps it was really his father's fault; even though Joe Sr. was one of the richest men in the country and was at one time head of the Securities and Exchange Commission, he forbade any of his children to talk about money at the dinner table.

When he appointed his brother Robert to the position of attorney general, he jokingly remarked that he wanted to see his little brother get some legal experience as a government lawyer before he had to go out into the real world and try his hands at private practice.

President:	**Lyndon B. Johnson**
Random goofy acts:	He won his first seat in the Senate by campaigning all over Texas in a helicopter. Every time he spotted someone (or a town or city) down below, he'd boom out over the copter's PA: "Hello down there. This is your friend, Lyndon Johnson."

As part of his drive to prove to the American people that the government could spend their money wisely, he would turn off every light in the White House he felt was burning unnecessarily. Unfortunately for everyone else, this meant that if they left their offices for even a few minutes they were likely to return to a dark room—not to mention a walk down a dark White House hallway bumping into other staff members and aides.

He often called spontaneous press conferences and had surprised journalists walk along with him as he gave them a briefing. The only problem was that he walked so fast everyone had to run to keep up with him—which made it hard to listen carefully, ask intelligent questions, or carry on a conversation. But he was a great fan of these fast-paced press conferences, which he called "Walkie-Talkies."

LBJ was also famous for holding meetings while he was sitting on the "throne" (if you catch our drift).

President:	**Richard Nixon**
Random goofy acts:	According to a former Secret Service agent, when Nixon went to the doctor he liked to put the hospital gown on backward and "tramp down the hall with the front flying open. The nurses would stop in their tracks."
	Once, just before doing an interview with David Frost, he turned to Frost and asked: "Well, did you do any fornicating this weekend?"
	While speaking at a Junior Chamber of Commerce meeting, he reflected on a trip he once made to Caracas, Venezuela, where he had been pelted by stones: "I got stoned in Caracas," he said. "I'll tell you one thing; it's a lot different from getting stoned at a Jaycee convention."

GOOFBALLS!

President:	**Gerald Ford**
Random goofy acts:	Rumor has it he showed up for his wedding with a brown shoe on one foot and a black shoe on the other.

One night when he took his dog out for a walk, he discovered he had locked himself out of the White House. Just as he resigned himself to the fact he was going to have to spend the night outside in his robe and slippers, a guard discovered him and let him back in.

His wife, Betty, once woke up and heard him talking in his sleep: "Thank you, thank you, thank you, thank, you, thank you," he said over and over again. When she woke him, he told her he had again been dreaming of standing in a receiving line.

President:	**Jimmy Carter**
Random goofy acts:	When he was a boy, he took his mother's diamond engagement ring to school and gave it to his teacher, Mrs. Forrest, with this explanation: "My daddy can always buy Momma another one."

Fifty-four years after FDR's first "Fireside Chat," he tried to duplicate FDR's success, appearing on television in the Oval Office beside a roaring fire, wearing a cardigan sweater instead of the traditional presidential suit. While his fireside chat may not have gone over as well as FDR's did, it did earn him a new nickname: "Jimmy Cardigan." He also tried his hand at communicating with the people via a call-in TV talk show called *Ask Mr. Carter.* For two hours he took calls from the American people. A total of nine million people called to ask a question of the president; only forty-two callers actually got through.

President:	**Ronald Reagan**
Random goofy acts:	He was named West Coast Father of the Year in 1976—the same year he forbade daughter Patti from bringing her boyfriend home because the two were living in sin.

As a sportscaster for WHO in Des Moines, he would fake the play-by-play of Chicago Cubs games by making up the plays as he read a news ticker tape. One day the ticker tape died mid-game, so he had to improvise. For six minutes he had the batter swing at pitch after pitch and sent each hit over the foul line until the ticker tape began to run again and he could return to reporting on the actual game.

President:	**George H. W. Bush**
Random goofy acts:	According to the book *Marching In Place, The Status Quo Presidency of George Bush* by *Time* magazine White House correspondents Michael Duffy and Dan Goodgame, George Bush elevated goofballness to an art form:

While running for president in 1988, he spent Halloween night running through his campaign airplane wearing a rubber George Bush mask and shouting "Read my lips! Read my lips!"

He once invited *Saturday Night Live*'s Dana Carvey to the White House so the comedian who had become famous impersonating him could do his impersonation to his face. Soon, both Bush and Carvey were "doing Bush" at one another. And when, as Duffy and Goodgame say, Carvey began "chopping the air with one hand and talking about 'Daaaan Quaaaaayle—getting stronger, learning ev-er-y daaay,' Bush doubled over in laughter. . . . By the end of 1991 Bush was doing imitations-of-Carvey-doing-imitations-of-Bush during televised press conferences."

GOOFBALLS!

Playing games and having a good time was a great Bush pastime. One of his favorite games as president was called "Light 'em up." Say Duffy and Goodgame:

> After taking the oath of office, Bush resembled nothing so much as a medieval boy king who woke up one morning, found himself atop the throne, and began tugging at the bell ropes for servants, ordering up royal carriages, and scheduling banquets and tournaments. . . . A delighted Bush single-handedly organized an all–White House horseshoe pitching contest, drawing up some of the ladders himself. . . . Bush's ebullience seemed limitless—as hundreds of local congressmen and political officials who attempted to buttonhole him during a presidential visit to their states would discover. Most solons try to put to good use the brief ride from the local airport into town, making a pitch for help with a local project or a hand in solving a snarled political problem. Bush, however, often preempted such appeals with an adult car game called "Light 'em up." In the back of his armored Cadillac limousine, Bush faced forward with his guest on the jump seat facing aft. As the limo moved through the streets, Bush would pick out someone from the crowd, usually an attractive woman or child, point, and wait until—pow!—eye contact and the victim realizes, He's looking at me! That's when the target "lit up." Because the limo was moving forward, it fell to the guest facing aft to report to the president when he asked, "Did I get her? Did I light her up?" And then the game would begin again.

He didn't inhale . . . and he didn't swallow either.

President:	**Bill Clinton**

Random goofy acts: In 1996 scientists came to the conclusion that chocolate can affect the same part of the brain that is turned on by smoking marijuana. When Clinton was asked to comment, he explained that he had once tried some chocolate . . . but didn't swallow.

In February of 1994, Clinton visited a truck plant in Louisiana. In the course of his visit, he spoke to the workers of the plant, and in his remarks he recounted that his first vehicle had been a truck. But he didn't leave it at that. Instead, as the *New York Times* tells it, "Mr. Clinton confided that he had lined the truck bed with Astroturf, adding with a sly grin, 'You don't want to know why.'" Well, of course we all wanted to know why—but the next day the only explanation Clinton could give (other than the obvious one) was that he'd covered the truck bed with Astroturf so he could haul luggage in it. "It wasn't for what everybody thought it was for when I made the comment, I'll tell you that. I'm guilty of a lot of things, but I didn't ever do that."

While Clinton was running his first presidential campaign in 1991, he was once asked the simple questions, "Do you watch much TV as you campaign across the country, and if so, what do you watch?" Here's what the president some called "Slick Willie" had to say:

> I'm not a big television watcher because I don't have much time to do it. So I do spend a lot of time doing it but normally I watch news programs and sports programs, and sometimes I come in very late at night and I'm all keyed up and I don't go to sleep, so I watch movies. . . . Sometimes I'll see *60 Minutes*

221

GOOFBALLS!

or *20/20*, but I'm usually away. As a matter of fact, my staff, when I'm on the road, will tape the early network news so I can watch it when I get home. . . . I watch CNN a lot.

As you can see, President Clinton was not a big television watcher because he didn't have much time to do it. But he spent a lot of time doing it, as you can see.

President:	**George W. Bush**
Random goofy act:	Those who know him know that George W. Bush loves to give a nickname to just about everyone he meets:

Karl Rove, deputy chief of staff: "Boy Genius" and "Turd Blossom"

Condoleezza Rice, secretary of state: "Guru"

Karen Hughes, adviser: "Lima Green Bean" and "High Prophet"

Dick Cheney, vice president: "Big Time"

Andrew Card, former chief of staff: "Tangent Man"

Vladimir Putin: "Pootie-Poot" and "Ostrich Legs"

Tony Blair, British prime minister: "Landslide"

Jean Chrétien, ex-Canadian prime minister: "Dino" (short for "Dinosaur")

Former President Bush: "41"

Barbara Bush: "No. 1"

First Lady Laura Bush: "Bushie" and "First"

Donald Rumsfeld, defense secretary: "Rummy"

Colin Powell, ex-secretary of state - "Baloonfoot"

Paul O'Neill, ex-Treasury secretary: "Big O"

George Tenet, ex-CIA director: "Brother George"

GOOFBALL HALL OF FAME

Historians love to rate and rank our presidents. And when it comes to assessing which were the most successful and which were the biggest failures, their conclusions are pretty predictable.

- Nominees for Best President are consistently Washington, Jefferson, Lincoln, Roosevelt, and Roosevelt.
- Nominees for Worst President are consistently Harding, Harding, Harding, Buchanan, and Grant.

Of course, when perusing these ratings it is always important to consider the source. And the criteria.

For instance, we happen to think George Washington was a horrible president. And if you thumb back through this book you'll see why: He was a boring old fart who made absolutely no effort toward providing the media with grist for their headline mills. No affairs, no scandals, no corruption—he didn't even drink too much or fight with his wife. How much fun was that for the American public?

And we're not the only one who says so. Nathaniel Hawthorne came to the same conclusion, wondering if "anyone has ever seen Washington in the nude. . . . It is inconceivable. He had no nakedness, but was born with his clothes on, and his hair powdered, and made a stately bow on his first appearance in the world." And Emerson concurred: "Every hero becomes a bore at last. . . . They cry up the virtues of George Washington—Damn George Washington!"

Washington—historians can have him.

GOOFBALLS!

Harding, on the other hand, is our kind of guy. His life was a mess. He had two mistresses, an illegitimate child, a handful of friends in appointed positions who were robbing the country blind, and he was totally unfit for the job. (And he was the first to admit it.) And to cap it all off, his vice president, Calvin Coolidge, was every bit the goofball he was.

Warren Harding just wanted to have fun. So he got himself elected president because, hey!, who has more toys and time and fun than the leader of the entire Western world?

Finally, Warren Harding's our kind of guy because he broke all the rules (objective, moral, constitutional, biblical, etc.), had a great time doing it, yet did such a great job of manipulating the nation and the press that the people were convinced he was a patriot, a great leader—hell, almost a saint—when he died.

The More Things Change

Well, the *New York Times* certainly showed the world what it thought of Warren G. Harding at the time of his nomination: "The firm and perfect flower of the cowardice and imbecility of the senatorial cabal."

The paper reversed its opinion four months later and proclaimed that he was "gradually assuming undisputed leadership."

Did We Mention . . .

As president, Harding ran up a debt
with his stockbroker of about
two hundred thousand dollars.
And then he died.

One of Warren Harding's favorite activities as
president was to visit the Gayety Burlesque,
which provided him with a special box seat
where he could see but couldn't be seen.

Perhaps *lazy* is the wrong word. Harding actually kept quite a rigorous
schedule:

- He played table tennis every morning.
- He played tennis every afternoon.
- He played golf two days a week.
- He played poker two nights a week.
- At noon every day he took time for a little constitutional,
  which also gave him an opportunity to shake hands with
  White House visitors.

GOOFBALLS!

Harding on Harding

"I am not fit for this office and
should never have been here."

—

"Oftentimes, as I sit here, I don't
seem to grasp that I am president."

—

"Jud, you have a college education, haven't
you? I don't know what to do or where to turn
on this taxation matter. Somewhere there
must be a book that tells all about it, where
I could go to straighten it out in my mind.
But I don't know where the book is, and
maybe I couldn't read it if I found it!"

VICE-GOOFBALL

WHAT'RE THE ODDS?

You take a guy like Warren Harding, goofball par excellence, and you've got to wonder where (or how) he could ever find a vice president goofy enough to complement his lying, cheating, lazy, goofball ways. But Harding did it again; he achieved the impossible.

His name was Calvin Coolidge.

In contrast to Warren Harding, Calvin Coolidge was an honest, hardworking family man who filled the role of president quite competently. He took office following Harding's death in 1923 and was reelected in 1924. In his five and a half years in office Coolidge reduced the national debt by about $2 billion. He reduced federal taxes three times and cleaned up Harding's fiscal messes by attacking the U.S. budget system and tinkering with it until it ran more smoothly.

Then, in 1928, while things were going along nicely and Americans everywhere were fat and happy and prosperous and Calvin Coolidge was an extremely popular man and it was assumed he would be easily reelected to a second term, he made this announcement to the press and the nation in typical Calvin Coolidge style: "I do not choose to run for president in 1928."

And that was all he said.

CALVIN SPEAKS!

His nickname was "Silent Cal." He was famous for saying . . . nothing.

- From an actual press conference with Calvin Coolidge:
  "Have you any statement on the campaign?"
  "No."
  "Can you tell us something about the world situation?"
  "No."

GOOFBALLS!

"Any information about Prohibition?"

"No . . . [And] remember—don't quote me."

- While Coolidge didn't think much of all the pomp and circumstance of Washington, he never turned down an invitation. Yet, once at a party or function he would talk as little as possible and leave by 10:00 p.m. When asked why he attended all these functions that he so obviously disliked, he replied, "Got to eat somewhere."
- While attending a dinner party, a woman seated near him bet she could get him to say three words. "You lose" was his only reply.
- A presidential aide once recalled a summons to the Oval Office by Coolidge one day. After arriving, the aide spent thirty minutes there in the room with the president— yet Silent Cal didn't say a word. Finally, confused, the aide got up to leave. When he reached the door Coolidge said, "Thank you for coming. I wanted to think."
- His first cabinet meeting after Harding's death lasted only fifteen minutes.

{"How could they tell?"}

—Dorothy Parker on the death
of Calvin Coolidge

CALVIN COOLIDGE—
A REAL BARREL OF FUN

- Calvin Coolidge's definition of fun? Riding the mechanical bucking horse he kept in his bedroom at the White House. He rode it almost every day.
- On his first day in the White House, Cal got so bored he called the same friend on the phone five times. Sometimes, when boredom set in, he would hit all the buttons on his desk at one time just to see everyone come running to see what was wrong.
- When Cal moved into the White House, he brought his own rocking chair; he liked to sit on the front porch and rock at night but quit after becoming annoyed with crowds of curious passersby.
- Coolidge loved to go fishing, but he made the Secret Service bait his hook.

A Real Wild Guy!

But don't start thinking of him as a daredevil. Given a choice, Cal always preferred that his chauffeur stick to a nice safe speed of about sixteen miles per hour.

GOOFBALLS!

"WHO YOU CALLIN' CHEAP?!"

Cal was not only famous for being tight with a word; he was also famous for being tight with a buck.

- When he was in the mood for a good cigar, Cal would reach for his stash of Fonseca Corona Fines deLuxe, which he got for twenty-one dollars per hundred. But when he wanted to share a cigar with a good friend, he had another stash of cigars . . . that cost him about three cents apiece.
- To save money, Coolidge tried to raise chickens at the White House. But for some reason, the chickens never tasted quite right. The mystery of the weird-tasting chickens was finally solved when someone pointed out that the chickens were penned right over the spot where Teddy Roosevelt had once grown mint.
- Cal liked to wander around the White House late at night—in his nightshirt. He often snuck into the kitchen and tried to figure out where all the White House leftovers had been stashed.
- Cal once drove a White House cook to quit because Cal didn't believe it would take six whole hams to feed sixty people at a state dinner.

THE FURTHER ADVENTURES OF CALVIN COOLIDGE

One day, an aide from the Library of Congress made a trip to the White House to arrange all the books in the library. As he sorted books Coolidge's dog kept nipping at his feet. Finally he got tired of shooing the dog away and did what anyone might do: He chucked a book at it. But he missed the dog, and the book bounced once and then hit something hard behind the curtain . . . and out stepped the president, who had been hiding.

"Warm day," Coolidge said, and quickly left the room.

Or Maybe Cal Wasn't So Goofy After All

"I should like to be known as a former president who tried to mind his own business."

—Calvin Coolidge

GOOFBALLS!

10
Veeps!*

"Once upon a time there was a farmer
who had two sons. One of them ran
off to sea. The other was elected vice
president of the United States. Nothing
was ever heard of either of them again."

—Thomas Marshall, vice president under Woodrow Wilson

*The word *Veep* was coined by the ten-year-old grandson of Vice President Alben Barkley.

Hᴇʀᴇ's ᴡʜʏ ɪᴛ's a rotten job:

It's a ticket to public ridicule, powerlessness, and—for most—eventual oblivion. Of the forty-six vice presidents who have served, only fourteen have gone on to be president (and only five of those VPs got elected president; the rest moved up from the VP seat because of death or resignation and then either refused to run again or ran and lost). As VP Thomas Marshall implies above, the rest have been sent out to pasture and have never been heard from again.

Let's face it. The job of vice president was an afterthought on the part of the Constitutional Convention, put into the works for only one reason: so that if the president died or was otherwise unable to perform his duties, there would be someone there to replace him without the need for a special election.

> "At a convintion nearly all th' dillygates lave as soon as they've nommyynated th' prisidint f'r fear wan iv thim will be mommyynated f'r vice presidint."
>
> —A political boss commenting in 1906 on the process of choosing a vice president

The Veep isn't part of the legislative branch of the government. Nor is he a member of the executive branch. And if you read the Constitution literally, he is neither the president's subordinate nor someone to whom the president can, as a matter of course, give orders.

234

WHITE HOUSE: CONFIDENTIAL

The vice president's only expressed responsibilities are:

- to preside over the Senate (but that doesn't mean he ever has to show up; most modern veeps physically preside over the Senate less than 2 percent of the time it is in session).
- to vote to break a tie (but he has no vote in the Senate at any other time).

As for unexpressed duties:

- He serves on the boards of the National Security Council and the Board of Regents of the Smithsonian Institution.
- He names a total of five cadets to the three military academies, and he appoints senators to such commissions as the Migratory Bird Conservation Commission.

Anything else he does during his term is at the request of the president.

Suddenly, the glamour of it all washes away. Unlike the job of president (which is what all veeps really want), the job of vice president begins to look like a dead end. But don't take our word for it. Let those who have served and those who have declined tell you in their own words.

Jurassic Veeps?

Vice President Thomas Marshall once summed up his job as a regent of the Smithsonian Institution by describing it as "an opportunity [for the vice president] to compare his fossilized life with the fossils of all ages."

"TELL HIM TO GO TO HELL"

—Truman's initial response when he
heard FDR wanted him to run as his VP

The room was crowded. Every damn political boss in the country was there, any of them you would want to name, and half a dozen governors.

And they all said, "Harry, we want you to be Vice President." I said, "I'm not going to do it."

Well, Bob Hannegan had put in a call to Roosevelt who was . . . down at San Diego. They finally got him on the phone. And with Roosevelt you didn't need a phone. All you had to do was raise the window and you could hear him.

I was sitting on one twin bed, and Bob was on the other in this room, and Roosevelt said [Mr. Truman gave a near-perfect imitation of Roosevelt, Harvard accent and all], Roosevelt said, "Bob, have you got that guy lined up yet on that vice Presidency?"

And Bob said, "No. He's the contrariest goddamn mule from Missouri I ever saw."

"Well," Roosevelt said, "you tell him if he wants to break up the Democratic Party in the middle of the war and maybe lose that war that's up to him."

—Harry Truman, in the book
*Plain Speaking: An Oral Biography
of Harry S Truman*

"My country, in its wisdom, contrived for me the most insignificant office that ever the invention of man contrived or his imagination conceived."

—John Adams,
America's first vice president

"Please accept my sincere sympathy."

—Telegram from Democratic vice president Marshall to newly nominated Republican VP candidate Calvin Coolidge

Much Ado About Not Much

Politics is power, and power can be summed up as the ability to spend and the ability to appoint. It should be noted, then, that in the 1880s the vice president had the power to make exactly four appointments: He could appoint his own secretary, his own private messenger, his own private telegraph operator, and—the appointment that was likely to be the most controversial—he had the power to appoint a restaurant-keeper for the Senate.

Mind Your Manners!

Even Harry's mom knew he was a contrary mule. The first time Harry phoned his mother after being inaugurated as vice president, she gave him these instructions: "Now, you behave yourself up there, Harry!"

VICE PRESIDENTIAL FOLLIES

- Vice President Hannibal Hamlin understood the significance of his job. Therefore, at the beginning of each new Senate session, he would spend a few weeks presiding over that body and then request that the Senate choose a president pro tempore to stand in for him so he could go home to his farm in Maine and do something useful.
- Vice President Richard Johnson, too, understood his place in the scheme of things. For that reason he took a leave of absence from his job as Veep so he could open and then manage a hotel, tavern, resort, and spa on his property in Kentucky.

{ "As useful as a cow's fifth teat." }

—Harry Truman on the vice presidency

WHITE HOUSE: CONFIDENTIAL

{ "A fifth wheel to a coach." }

—Teddy Roosevelt on the vice presidency

- Vice President John Nance Garner was given virtually nothing to do by FDR, so he spent most of his time at his ranch in Uvalde, Texas, sitting on his porch shooting at a spittoon. Years later, when fellow Texan LBJ asked Garner if he should accept the vice presidential nomination, Garner replied: "The vice presidency ain't worth a pitcher of warm spit."

{ "[Once, while visiting Denver] a big burly policeman kept following me around, until I asked him what he was doing. He said he was guarding my person. I said, 'Your labor is in vain. Nobody was ever crazy enough to shoot at a vice president. If you will go away and find somebody to shoot at me, I'll go down in history as being the first vice president who ever attracted enough attention even to have a crank shoot at him.'" }

—Vice President John Marshall

- LBJ and his aides never dreamed that in 1960 he would be JFK's running mate—as the *vice-presidential* candidate anyway. In fact, while Senator Kennedy crisscrossed the country stumping for the Democratic nomination, Johnson stayed in Washington; he was sure he'd get the nomination, and he felt his job as Senate majority leader required him to stay on the job.

  One of Johnson's aides was quoted as saying, "I can see it all now. Johnson will be standing in the hotel room after he wins the nomination, and he'll say, 'We want Sonny Boy for vice president. Go fetch him for me.'"

  When Kennedy won the nomination, Johnson explained his own loss this way: "Jack was out kissing babies while I was passing bills."

{"You die, I fly."}

—Then Vice President George H. W. Bush, making the
succinct observation that the job of VP consists mostly
of going to funerals when foreign dignitaries die

"Well, why don't you take the word *Quayle* and insert the word *Bush* wherever it appears, and that's the crap I took for eight years. Wimp. Sycophant. Lapdog. Poop. Lightweight. Boob. Squirrel. Asshole. George Bush."

—President George H. W. Bush takes a moment to console his own VP, Dan Quayle

THEY JUST SAID "NO!"

"I do not choose to be buried until I am really dead."

—Daniel Webster, explaining why he declined the
vice-presidential nomination in 1848

"I shall not, under any circumstances, consent to the employment of my name in connection with that office. Indeed should I be nominated for it by the convention, I would most assuredly decline. It is the very last office under the Government I would desire to hold."

—James Buchanan, declining the vice-presidential nomination in 1852
(Wise move—he was later elected president in 1856)

"Ask him what he [Abraham Lincoln] thinks I have done to deserve the punishment, at forty-six years of age, of being made to sit as presiding officer over the Senate, to listen to debates, more or less stupid, in which I can take no part nor say a word."

—Major General Benjamin F. Butler, declining the
vice-presidential nomination in 1864

THE (SECOND) BEST
AMERICA HAS TO OFFER!

ONE PARTY BOSS'S perspective on why Nixon was chosen as Eisenhower's running mate: "We took Dick Nixon not because he was right wing or left wing—but because we were tired and he came from California."

How underappreciated was Nixon by President Eisenhower? Near the end of Ike's last term, while Nixon was running his own presidential campaign, Ike was asked to give an example of one major idea of Nixon's that he as president had adopted. Ike's reply: "If you give me a week, I might think of one."

FIFTEEN MINUTES OF FAME

OCCASIONALLY A VICE president who is otherwise un-noteworthy from a historical perspective will commit one act or coin one phrase that will live far longer than the name of the man himself. Such is the case of Vice President Thomas Marshall, who, while sitting through a long windy speech entitled "What This Country Needs" by a senator, commented to a nearby aide so everyone in the Senate could hear: "What this country needs is a really good five-cent cigar."

THE ULTIMATE HUMILIATION, IN THEORY

IMAGINE WHAT IT'S like to be a vice president who has just lost a bid for the presidency: Because the VP is also the president of the Senate, it is his job to count the votes of the electoral college before all members of Congress and to announce the name of the next president. Therefore, if you are VP and you have just lost the election, you have to suffer the ultimate humiliation of announcing the winner—your opponent—to Congress and God and everyone.

Just another way our founding fathers designed the job so as to give it to the VP in the shorts.

THE ULTIMATE HUMILIATION, IN PRACTICE

IN THE 2000 presidential election, Al Gore appeared to have won the popular vote, but in Florida, the race came down to a few hundred votes, while there were also alleged irregularities over how the Florida votes were counted. And whoever won Florida would also have enough Electoral College votes to win the presidency.

A machine count was done, and it showed that George W. Bush was the winner by a close margin . . . but there were still those vote-counting irregularities hanging over the election returns.

In response, the Gore campaign insisted on a manual recount. The Bush campaign sued to prevent the recount. The Florida Supreme Court ruled that a recount *should* be done. And more than a month after the election, the U.S. Supreme Court ruled on a 5-4 vote that there should be *no* recount.

Of course, as the president of the Senate, Al Gore then had to go before that body and humiliate himself by anointing his opponent as the new president . . . even though he surely believed in his heart of hearts that he was really the guy who won the election.

"How Dare You Call Me That?!"

When Al Gore was running for president in 1988 (four years before he accepted Bill Clinton's invitation to run as VP), he publically and vociferously rebuffed a heckler for shouting what he considered to be the ultimate insult.

Did the heckler insult Gore's mother? Make reference to the state of marriage of Gore's parents at the time of his birth? Insult his wife and children?

Nope. The insult to which Gore took such offense was that he had all the traits of a really good vice president.

11

Executive Privilege(s)!

executive privilege n. The principle that members of the executive branch of government cannot legally be forced to disclose their confidential communications when such disclosure would adversely affect the operations or procedures of the executive branch.

—FROM THE AMERICAN HERITAGE® DICTIONARY
OF THE ENGLISH LANGUAGE, FOURTH EDITION

executive privilege(s)™ n. The principle that members of the executive branch of government, and their families and friends, cannot be expected to live by the same rules that folks like the rest of us do . . . because hey, this is the president and his friends and family we're talking about!

—FROM GREGG STEBBEN AND AUSTIN HILL,
A COUPLE OF JEALOUS SMART-ASSES

WHEN THE PRESIDENT (AND HIS LAWYERS) HIDE BEHIND EXECUTIVE PRIVILEGE, IT'S OFTEN A BUTT-COVERING MOVE OF DRAMATIC PROPORTIONS

And to you, our faithful reader, the two words *executive privilege* should be the sign of some wonderfully entertaining, fast-talking, fact-changing, history-revising, buck-passing madcap adventures to come from the White House.

After all, if you were the president and you *knew* you did nothing wrong, why would you bother invoking executive privilege?

Birds do it, bees do it... but not all presidents do it

Just in case you're wondering, there has been at least one president who lost not a single staff member or member of his administration to an indictment or scandal-related resignation. Ironically, it was FDR, who also served almost twice as long as any other president.

SELFISH SECRETS VS. SELFLESS SECRETS

THE CONSTITUTION CLEARLY spells out the powers to be possessed by each branch of the federal government, and the phrase *executive privilege* doesn't appear anywhere in the Constitution.

In fact, apart from mandating that the president must report to the congress on the "State of the Union" once a year, the Constitution doesn't really say ANYTHING about what kind of information the president has to divulge.

Hmmm.

Well, that's kind of a problem, isn't it? After all, even cynical authors like ourselves can imagine times when the president might know something that was best sheltered from all but a few members of Congress and the public, like, say:

- Matters of national security
- Matters that might adversely affect the economy
- Stupid stuff that shouldn't matter

On the other hand, we can also imagine lots of times when the president might be tempted to invoke executive privilege for all the *wrong* reasons: you know, like to cover his own butt, or to cover the butt of a family member or a political or personal friend.

{ "Every President since Washington has exercised some form of what we today call executive privilege, regardless of the words used to describe their actions." }

—Mark J. Rozell, professor of politics,
The Catholic University of America
in Washington D.C.

EXECUTIVE PRIVILEGE(S)!

Q: Who was the first president to invoke executive privilege?

a. Richard Nixon

b. Bill Clinton

c. Ray Akers

d. Thomas Jefferson

e. George Washington

(Go to the next page to discuss!)

DISCUSSION GROUP GUIDE FOR THE QUESTION
"WHO WAS THE FIRST PRESIDENT TO INVOKE EXECUTIVE PRIVILEGE?"

We can just see the wheels turning in your brain as you stew on this.

It's gotta be Richard Nixon, right?
After all, until he came along all our presidents were little angels.

No, maybe it's Bill Clinton.
Didn't he invent the whole concept of executive privilege, right after he invented the whole concept of multiple definitions of the word *is*?

No, no, no . . . it's gotta be George Washington.
After all, he was the first president (sort of, see Appendix C: The George Washington Conspiracy on page 321), and he must have needed it to protect himself when he otherwise would have had to tell a lie at a time when telling the truth would have been dangerous for this new nation and the American people. And you *know* that George Washington *never* told a lie (except in the case of the George Washington Conspiracy, which is on page 321).

Well, the one guy it couldn't be was Thomas Jefferson—he just wouldn't do that!
And besides . . . what would Thomas Jefferson ever have to hide?

(Go to next page for the answer)

EXECUTIVE PRIVILEGE(S)!

ANSWER TO THE QUESTION:

Q: SO, WHO <u>WAS</u> THE FIRST PRESIDENT TO INVOKE EXECUTIVE PRIVILEGE?

A: IT WAS THOMAS JEFFERSON.

And what did HE have to hide? Well, we're not sure, because he invented the concept of executive privilege and then used it to keep what he knew a secret. And it's still a secret, even to this day.

But what happened was that he was subpoenaed to testify and present documentation in the treason trial of his own vice president, Aaron Burr.

Of course, it could have been worse. Jefferson could have been subpoenaed to testify and present documentation in a *murder* trial against his own vice president after Burr shot and killed Alexander Hamilton in a duel, but Burr never stood trial for the murder, which everyone knew he committed.

252

And When Executive Privilege Is NOT Enough

After Vice President Aaron Burr shot and killed Alexander Hamilton in a duel, he didn't feel he needed to invoke executive privilege to protect himself.

Why?

Well, even though he was charged with murder in New York (where Hamilton died) and he was charged and acquitted in New Jersey (where the actual duel occurred), he knew that if he immediately raced to Washington D.C. following the duel, neither New York nor New Jersey would have the legal right to extradite him.

So off to D.C. he ran, and served out his term as vice president and president of the U.S. Senate as if the murder of Treasury Secretary Alexander Hamilton had never happened.

WHAT THE PRESIDENT DIDN'T SAY . . .
AND WHEN HE DIDN'T SAY IT

George Washington

After General Arthur St. Clair led an expedition against American Indian tribes along the Ohio River in which an entire division was lost, a congressional committee requested information about the tragedy from Washington. Initially, he wasn't sure how to respond and, depending on how he responded, what kind of legal precedent might be set.

So Washington called a meeting of his cabinet, closed the door behind them, and started asking them questions—and he didn't take any notes.

Fortunately, Thomas Jefferson wrote about the meeting in his personal diary, which is how we know about it today.

Apparently, according to Jefferson, the cabinet members agreed that the Congress had the right to request information from the president, and that the president "ought to communicate such papers as the public good would permit & ought to refuse those the disclosure of which would injure the public."

As for the immediate situation, the cabinet agreed that "there was not a paper which might not be properly produced," **so President Washington handed over the information that Congress was asking for, and that was that.**

Then George Washington faced a Congressional request in 1794 to see the president's correspondence with his Ambassador to France . . . because the ambassador to France was suspected of aiding the French aristocrats against the revolutionaries despite the United States' official stance of neutrality in the French Revolution. **Washington handed over the letters, but not without censoring them first.**

And a year later, in 1795, Congress asked for information about a treaty being negotiated with Great Britain. **This time, however, Washington flat-out told them "no," and he explained that the House of Representatives had no constitutional authority to participate in negotiating treaties and thus did not need to see any information about it.**

EXECUTIVE PRIVILEGE(S)!

This didn't quite qualify as invoking executive privilege, however. It was more a case of clarifying the rules of the game. (Besides, as you are about to see, Jefferson hadn't "invented" executive privilege yet.)

Thomas Jefferson

Not only did he invent the dumbwaiter, and the first copy machine, and baked Alaska, he also invented executive privilege. Jefferson knew stuff about his veep Aaron Burr, that rat fink (and murderer and traitor), that he didn't want to talk about, **so he cooked up the whole "executive privilege" concept as a way to justify withholding information.**

By the way, Jefferson was the first president to use executive privilege a second time, too, which he did **when he and his secretary of state, James Madison, tried to get Congress to give them $2 million to buy some Florida swamp lands from the Spanish before the French could get their hands on it.**

As for why Jefferson and Madison wanted to keep the deal a secret from Congress, well, that's a story we'll save for our next book, *U.S. Foreign Policy: Confidential.*

Andrew Jackson

In 1832 when Andrew Jackson set out to destroy the Second Bank of the United States, he had a clash with Congress over demands for info. **Jackson believed that his political opponents' demands amounted to petty partisan harassment, so he used executive privilege to resist their demands for information.**

Grover Cleveland

He **refused to hand over files to Congress pertaining to presidential appointments** because he believed the requests were politically motivated.

{ There are only two occasions when Americans respect privacy, especially in Presidents. Those are prayer and fishing. }

—Herbert Hoover

Dwight D. Eisenhower

Ike to Congress: "Yes, I've got a secret . . . but I'm not telling!" Before President Eisenhower's days in the White House, presidents were almost always willing to cough up a good reason why they should be allowed to withhold information and "keep secrets."

And they had some great reasons, too: They needed to safeguard foreign policy discussions; they needed to "keep the confidence" of certain people and groups; "innocent people" might get hurt; or maybe they just wanted to avoid getting in to big nasty political fights. (Okay, maybe that last reason was kind of lame, but you could still see why it would be important to the president). Eisenhower, on the other hand, really wanted to expand the president's ability to withhold information from Congress.

Why?

Because following World War II, the Cold War era seemed to require that the presidency be allowed to function with more secrecy, given the threat of Soviet dominance in the world. Or to say it another way, it seemed to be necessary for the presidency to function as though it were at war, even though the war was, well, "cold."

On May 17 1954, President Eisenhower sent a letter to his Secretary of Defense instructing department officials to not cooperate with the Congress in their demands for information regarding the investigation of the army by Senator Joseph McCarthy. And since most Americans took the Cold War seriously, and since many in the Congress didn't like the infamous Senator McCarthy, nobody complained too much about Eisenhower's secrecy.

Later in the Eisenhower presidency, his Attorney General William Rogers would officially use the term *executive privilege* for the first time. **And before he left office, President Eisenhower would have asserted executive privilege no fewer than forty times.**

$\left\{\begin{array}{c}\text{"Don't worry, Jim. If it comes up,}\\ \text{I'll just confuse them."}\end{array}\right\}$

—President Eisenhower to his press secretary,
just before a press conference

EXECUTIVE PRIVILEGE(S)!

JFK & LBJ

Despite the fact that Eisenhower managed to get away with dramatically strengthening the presidency, some in Congress didn't like all this executive privilege secrecy stuff. So, beginning with the Kennedy administration, Congress began a new precedent of sending the president a formal letter and asking for his official policy on executive privilege.

President Kennedy wrote back, explaining that executive privilege can be invoked only by the president (as opposed to other members of the executive branch). President Johnson similarly replied that only the president would assert executive privilege.

Richard Nixon

Well, it seemed like a good idea at the time. . . .

When President Nixon got that executive privilege letter from Congress, he responded in the greatest detail, stating that "the scope of executive privilege must be very narrowly construed. Under this Administration, executive privilege will not be asserted without specific presidential approval . . . I want open government to be a reality in every way possible."

But when the Senate began investigating Watergate, things really got ugly. **Nixon at that point began using the assertion of executive privilege as a means to prevent his aides from testifying before Congress,** and to avoid handing over his now-famous White House tape recordings.

{ "I don't give a shit what happens. I want you all to stonewall it, let them plead the Fifth Amendment, cover-up, or anything else, if it'll save it—save the plan. That's the whole point." }

—Richard Nixon, on one of his infamous Watergate tapes, which he tried to keep from Congress by invoking executive privilege

Gerald Ford

Maybe he thought it was just another credit card offer. . . .

When that congressional letter arrived asking about his "official policy" on executive privilege, he didn't even answer it.

Why?

Because he realized that the terms *executive privilege* and *Watergate* had become synonymous in the minds of many Americans (duh!), so **rather than offer an official policy on the matter, he chose to handle information-withholding matters on a case-by-case basis.**

Jimmy Carter

Oddly enough, Jimmy Carter didn't address the issue of executive privilege until just days before he lost reelection.

Ronald Reagan

The first Reagan-era assertion of executive privilege came in 1981, before Reagan's administration had offered an official position on executive privilege.

Congress had asked Reagan's Interior Secretary James Watt for some documentation on environmental matters, and Watt refused, claiming that they were highly "sensitive."

This turned in to a political fiasco, so finally the Administration orchestrated a "compromise" and after nearly two years in office, issued an official document outlining its position on executive privilege.

And their position was?

That they were committed to complying with congressional information requests, but that some communications needed to remain confidential.

George Herbert Walker Bush

Read his lips: He never invoked the term *executive privilege* . . . but that doesn't mean his administration never withheld information that was requested.

EXECUTIVE PRIVILEGE(S)!

Bill Clinton

Travel-gate!

In 1996, President Clinton claimed executive privilege in withholding documents subpoenaed during the investigation of the firing of White House travel office workers in 1994. Attorney General Janet Reno offered her legal opinion, agreeing with the president that **it was a legitimate use of executive privilege.**

Monica-gate!

In 1998, President Clinton invoked executive privilege and **attempted to block prosecutors from questioning his senior aides** in the independent counsel investigation of "obstruction of justice" claims.

Hillary-gate!

In 1999, President Clinton extended clemency to sixteen members of a Puerto Rican nationalist group, people who were considered to be terrorists, and to be dangerous, by the federal government. **Congress asked to review documents concerning the individuals granted clemency, and Clinton rejected the request, claiming executive privilege.**

Many of President Clinton's foes argued that by extending this clemency, the president was sacrificing national security for the sake of "kissing ass" with New York's large population of citizens who are of Puerto Rican descent—and that this was an attempt to "buy Puerto Rican votes" for his wife's senate campaign.

> "You know, the clock is running down on the Republicans in Congress, too. I feel for them. I do. . . . They've only got seven more months to investigate me. That's a lot of pressure. So little time, so many unanswered questions. For example, over the last few months, I've lost ten pounds. Where did they go? Why haven't I produced them to the independent counsel? How did some of them manage to wind up on Tim Russert [the host of NBC's *Meet the Press*]?
>
> —Bill Clinton at his last White House Correspondents' Dinner as president, poking fun at his own ability to get himself in trouble as well as the Republican Congress' determined efforts to catch him and nail him whenever they could

George W. Bush

In early 2001, Bush stated publicly that he wanted to put an end to the various Clinton scandal investigations . . . and then he refused to hand over documents to Congress when it sought to subpoena records concerning Department of Justice decision-making by Bill Clinton's Attorney General, Janet Reno.

When President Bush chose Harriet Miers (more on her later) as a Supreme Court nominee, he was asked by both Republicans and Democrats to hand over information about meetings and consultations with her. **He refused, claiming that such things needed to remain private since she had at one time been his own personal attorney.**

In an incident involving Vice President Dick Cheney, **the vice president refused to hand over information about who was in attendance at various meetings of his "energy task force."** The veep didn't use the words *executive privilege* when defending his withholding of information, but nonetheless he used legal language that looked a lot like a defense of executive privilege. Cheney's actions were also a break from the common understanding that executive privilege is intended for the president and only the president. Bush foes were incensed at this attempt to cover up who was part of the Bush administration's "energy task force," given the president and vice president's close ties to the oil and energy industry before taking office.

BEING THE PRESIDENT, OR THE PRESIDENT'S FRIEND, OR A FAMILY MEMBER . . . AND GETTING AWAY WITH ALL KINDS OF STUFF BECAUSE OF IT?

PRICELESS.

FOR EVERYTHING ELSE . . .
THERE'S EXECUTIVE PRIVILEGE(S)™.

Hey, stuff happens.

Even to presidents. And their friends. And their families.

We know that; we're understanding guys.

And that's why, in the course of writing this book, we invented the "Executive Privilege(s)™ card" . . . because there are times (like the following examples) when a chief executive (or someone close to him) does something kind of dumb but not TOO serious, that *doesn't necessarily* or *gravely* affect national security, domestic policy, or other matters of great import, but it's serious enough that he needs the equivalent of a "Get Out of Jail Free" card with a whopping-high credit limit to get himself (or the friend or family member) out of trouble when they've done something really stupid.

"WE JUST DROPPED THE BOMB ON RUSSIA . . . NEWS AT 11"

Ir was the middle of the Cold War, and President Reagan told us Russia was the "Evil Empire."

And then one day in 1984, while preparing for his weekly radio addresses, without realizing the microphone in front of him was on, the president made a clever joke of an announcement to amuse himself:

"My fellow Americans, I'm pleased to tell you today that I've signed legislation that will outlaw Russia forever. We begin bombing in five minutes."

261

This little "joke" caused an immediate alteration in the "DEFCON" (Defense Condition) level and created one of the tensest moments of the entire Cold War.

EXECUTIVE PRIVILEGE(S)!

U.S. PRESIDENT TO ENTIRE NATION OF AUSTRALIA:

"F**K YOU!"

WHILE VISITING AUSTRALIA, President Richard Nixon wanted to get off *Air Force One* looking very statesman-like, so he did something he had seen Winston Churchill do many times during World War II: He flashed the "peace sign."

What Nixon didn't know was that in Australia, there are a couple of different meanings for what he knew as the "peace sign."

In Australia, when the gesture is offered with the palm of one's hand pointing *outward,* it means "peace." But when the sign is displayed with the palm facing *inward,* as Nixon did it, it means "f**k you" or "f**k off" . . . which was the message President Nixon sent to awaiting Australian dignitaries and the entire nation of Australia by television as he deplaned from *Air Force One* with a smile on his face and one offending hand gesturing enthusiastically.

FOUR ABOVE THE LAW . . .

Sometimes, presidents need to pull out their mighty Executive Privilege(s)™ card and *literally* use it as a "Get-Out-of-Jail-Free" card:

- As president, William Howard Taft once got caught picking flowers outside the Department of Agriculture building, and he would have been arrested if the watchman hadn't recognized him and let him go.
- When LBJ got busted for speeding while in Texas, the officer gasped and said, "Oh, my God!" when he realized who he had pulled over . . . to which LBJ replied: "And don't you forget it."
- President Franklin Pierce (who was famous for having a drinking problem) was once arrested for running an old woman down on the streets of Washington in his carriage, but he could never be proven guilty, so the case was closed.
- After a police officer pulled Ulysses S. Grant over for using excessive speed while traveling through Washington D.C. in a horse and carriage, the officer decided not to write the president a ticket. Grant, on the other hand, insisted that the officer do his duty and issue the ticket anyway.

. . . AND ONE FOR UNDER THE TABLE

Warren Harding loved to serve his friends lots of hard liquor during their infamous weekly White House poker games, and no one thought it was a problem, even though Harding was president during Prohibition when the possession of alcohol was a crime.

And for one president a "Get-INTO-Jail" card

Of course, nobody likes being criticized, but President John Adams was particularly sensitive about it. Which may be one reason why he signed into law the "Alien & Sedition Acts," which made it possible for anyone who was critical of the government to be thrown into jail.

VEEP GETS DRUNK WITH POWER
(OR JUST GETS DRUNK)

ACCORDING TO SENATOR William Stewart of Nevada, who was there at the time:

> He (Vice President–elect Andrew Johnson) came to Washington in January or February, 1865, and for some weeks previous to the inauguration of President Lincoln on the 4th of March, 1865, his general condition was a half-drunken stupor. When he entered the Senate chamber to take the oath of office as Vice President, and to call that body to order, he was very drunk. He was assisted to the chair by the Sergeant-at-Arms and two door-keepers, and was unable to stand without assistance. I do not believe he was conscious when he took the oath of office.
>
> Immediately after the oath had been administered, he grasped the desk before him with an unsteady hand, and, swaying about so that he threatened to tumble down at any moment, he began an incoherent tirade. . . . Finally he was removed, not without some force, by the Sergeant-at-Arms to the Vice-President's room, where he was detained until the ceremony was concluded.

And now, for the official White House spin on the story:

Johnson was sick with typhoid fever, took a few slugs of whiskey to get him through the ceremony, and it went straight to his head.

{ I have known Andy Johnson for many years; he made a bad slip the other day, but you need not be scared; Andy ain't a drunkard." }

—Abe Lincoln

IF IT'S THE "PEOPLE'S HOUSE," DOESN'T THAT MEAN THEY'RE ALSO THE "PEOPLE'S DISHES"???

WHEN FOLKS LIKE you or us play a little poker, we use the money in our wallet, then the money in our bank accounts, then the good credit extended to us on our credit cards. And then, if we're crazy enough, we start betting things like the deeds on our houses.

Unfortunately, in his weekly poker games with his "poker cabinet," President Warren Harding couldn't bet *his* house, because he lived at the White House.

So he did the next best thing: In a single hand, he bet and lost an entire set of White House china that dated back to the presidency of Benjamin Harrison. The value of the dishes, of course, was probably priceless.

FURNITURE-GATE???

Look, WE THINK it's kind of silly too, but back in the early days of the presidency, every president had his own "Presidential Furniture Fund" which was granted by Congress to enable the president to—what else?—buy furniture.

Now, to be fair, this was after the British burned the White House to the ground, so as silly as it sounds now, it actually made sense at the time. And believe it or not, the "Presidential Furniture Fund" was the source of several "grand" scandals:

WHY U.S. PRESIDENTS NEVER SHOP AT IKEA:

It all started with Dolley Madison, who spent forty dollars to buy an imported mirror for the White House. Members of the Senate were furious and launched an investigation that cost several thousand dollars to complete.

So, why were members of the Senate so upset? Well, it wasn't because of the forty-dollar price tag on the mirror. It was because Dolley had dared to buy a decoration for the White House that had been imported from another country.

CAN YOU SAY "TRAVEL-GATE," PRESIDENT MONROE?

James Monroe got in trouble over the "Presidential Furniture Fund" when he borrowed money from the fund to pay for some presidential travel.

Okay, maybe this wasn't so bad, except that Monroe's enemies accused him of using the money to finance trips that were made for Monroe's own political gain.

"WE GOT TROUBLE, MY FRIENDS! RIGHT HERE IN CAPITAL CITY!"

Everyone, now—sing along with *The Music Man*:
> Well, ya got trouble,
> Right here in River city!
> With a capital *T*
> And that rhymes with *P*
> And that stands for *Pool!*

But we're guessing no one took John Quincy Adams to see *The Music Man* or told him about the grave dangers of the game, because it turns out he used part of his "Presidential Furniture Fund" to buy a chess set and a billiards table.

And yes, as you might imagine, when he was running for reelection, his opponent smeared him with the claim that he had used taxpayer money to buy "gambling furniture."

> "It would stink in the nostrils of the American people to have it said the President of the United States had approved a bill overrunning an appropriation of $20,000 for flub-dubs for this damned old house, when the soldiers cannot have blankets."

— Abe Lincoln to wife Mary, after finding out she had exceeded her Congressional $20,000 White House decorating budget by $6,700

EXECUTIVE PRIVILEGE(S)!

DOES MCI/WORLDCOM HAVE AN OPENING FOR A "FIRST LADY" WITH EXPERIENCE IN ACCOUNTING?

NOT ONLY DID Mary Todd Lincoln get caught going over her Congressional decorating budget when buying "flub-dubs" for the White House, she also intentionally overcharged the government on her White House expense account.

Of course, we must caution you not to try this at home (or at work!), but here's how she did it:

> While preparing a state banquet for France's Emperor Napoleon III she billed the Interior Department nine hundred dollars, when in fact the event only cost three hundred dollars.

And here's how she did it again:

> When the secretary of the interior rejected these charges, Mrs. Lincoln had a gardener fake a bill for plants and flowers; then she certified the bill herself, and pocketed the excess money.

All this was bad news for poor "Honest Abe" Lincoln, of course, particularly as the Civil War was raging on and many in the Union were making tremendous personal sacrifices for the good of the country.

JACKIE KENNEDY KILLS THE $45,000-A-YEAR MYTH

WHILE JACK KENNEDY was campaigning for the presidency, the owner and publisher of *Women's Wear Daily* reported that the candidate's wife Jackie spent $45,000 per year on clothes.

Jackie, of course, knew the truth and replied, with typical wit and aplomb: "I couldn't do that without wearing sable underwear!"

But when she moved into the White House and became the First Lady, her clothing allowance, in fact, escalated to $121,000 in the year 1962 alone!

You might also be interested to know that when Congress refused to give John Tyler's wife Julia any money to redecorate the White House, she decided to use her own money to add her own style of "flub-dubs" to the place.

FOR WHAT IT'S WORTH

NANCY REAGAN HAD quite an appetite for nice clothes too, but she didn't have access to the same kind of money that Jackie did. However she did somehow manage to "borrow" lots of *really* expensive gowns and dresses from designers, even though she often "forgot" to give them back.

This was a problem for two reasons:

1. The First Lady is not supposed to accept expensive gifts (which they ostensibly were, if she never returned the clothes on loan).
2. If the clothes were gifts instead of loans, the First Lady *should* have been claiming the gifts on her taxes, which she never did.

In the end, Nancy announced in 1982 that she would stop borrowing gowns and dresses from designers, but that didn't stop the IRS from hitting her with a million-dollar tax bill for all the dresses she had "borrowed" but never returned.

270

{ "Haven't you seen an old lady
walk a dog before?" }

—First Lady Barbara Bush to gawking reporters,
as she took her dog Millie out for a walk
in a bathrobe and slippers

HELEN TAFT THROWS A MILLION-DOLLAR PARTY

William Howard Taft's wife Helen was quite the social climber—even being First Lady was not enough for her.

So when the 25th anniversary of her wedding to the president rolled around, she decided to invite four thousand of her closest friends to the White House to celebrate the occasion.

But here's where the story starts to get interesting: Helen worded the party invitations in such a way that it was obvious to guests that bringing an expensive gift was a requirement for getting through the door. At the party, guests wandered around the White House grounds asking each other how much they had spent on a gift to get in. And in the end, the Tafts ended up taking in more than a million dollars' worth of silver in gifts that evening.

On the Other Hand:

When Eleanor Roosevelt threw a party for the queen . . . she served hot dogs!

PRESIDENT PARDONS PIRATE??

WELL, YEAH . . . BUT at least he was OUR pirate.

This all dates back to the War of 1812, when the British tried to get to get pirate Jean Laffite to help them take over New Orleans.

But Jean was a very wily pirate, of course, so he accepted an offer from President James Madison to fight on the U.S. side in exchange for a pardon for himself and his men.

Jean Laffite and his men fought nobly for the United States. Then after the war, Laffite and his fellow pirates took their pardons along with their pirate ships, moved down the coast to Galveston, Texas, and went back to terrorizing U.S. citizens and others as they resumed their pirating, looting ways.

PRESIDENT PARDONS PORN STAR???

WELL, NOT EXACTLY.

But in 1981 President Reagan did pardon a former FBI agent by the name of Mark Felt for giving FBI agents authorization to break into the offices of Vietnam protestors without warrants.

Today, of course, we know that Mark Felt was leading a double life during the Nixon presidency, because while by day he was the number two man at the FBI, by night he was feeding information about Watergate to Woodward and Bernstein at the *Washington Post.*

Woodward and Bernstein gave Mark Felt the nickname "Deep Throat" because around the same time the FBI agent was insisting that that everything he shared with them be kept as "deep background," a notorious porn movie called *Deep Throat* and its star Linda Lovelace were front and center in the news.

But did Reagan *know* he was pardoning "Deep Throat"?

Even if he didn't, surely some of his aides must have suspected as much . . . because Mark Felt had always been an obvious guy to point a finger at, despite his own protestations that he was *not* the leak known as "Deep Throat."

"WELL, EXCUUUUSE ME!"

WE INTERRUPT THIS CHAPTER FOR A FEW WORDS
ABOUT PRESIDENTIAL PARDONS*

If you think about it, the ULTIMATE executive privilege is having the right to wave a magic wand and make someone's guilt go away (in the eyes of the law). William H. Harrison and James Garfield pardoned no one. But of course, Harrison was president for only a month before he died, and Garfield had been president less than four months when he was shot and later died. George Washington only pardoned 16 people, John Adams only pardoned 21 people, and George H. W. Bush only pardoned 77 people. On the other hand, FDR pardoned 3,687 people (although he was in office almost twice as long as anyone else); Woodrow Wilson pardoned 2,480 people, and Harry Truman pardoned 2,044. But sometimes the real story is hiding behind the statistics:

Year	Backstory
1795	George Washington granted amnesty to the Whiskey Rebellion rebels.
1868	Andrew Johnson granted amnesty to the Confederate rebels.
1869	Andrew Johnson also pardoned Samuel Mudd, the doctor who set the broken leg of John Wilkes Booth after he assassinated Abraham Lincoln.
1971	Richard Nixon commuted the sentence of former Teamsters boss Jimmy Hoffa.
1977	Gerald Ford pardoned Tokyo Rose.
1977	Jimmy Carter granted amnesty to Vietnam draft evaders.
1979	Jimmy Carter commuted the sentence of Patty Hearst for her role in an armed robbery.
2000	Bill Clinton pardoned former Congressman Dan Rostenkowski, who was guilty of misusing taxpayer dollars.
2001	Bill Clinton pardoned Marc Rich, who had been indicted of evading more than $48 million in taxes. He was also charged with fifty-one counts of tax fraud and with running illegal oil deals with Iran during the hostage crisis.

*We're using the word *pardon* quite broadly here and including amnesty, commuted sentences, and other forms of clemency in our count.

EXECUTIVE PRIVILEGE(S)!

TRUMAN SAVES OWN ASSASSIN FROM DEATH!

In 1950, two Puerto Rican nationals attempted to kill President Truman as a way to call attention to the cause of Puerto Rican independence.

The assassination attempt failed, and one of the gunmen (Griselio Torresola) was killed. The other gunman, Oscar Collazo, was tried and sentenced to death, but one week before his scheduled execution in 1952, President Truman commuted his sentence to life imprisonment.

WHAT DOES RICHARD NIXON HAVE IN COMMON WITH JIMMY HOFFA?

1. Just like Jimmy Hoffa, Richard Nixon was the recipient of a presidential pardon (thanks to Gerald Ford, in 1974).
2. And just like Jimmy Hoffa, Richard Nixon spent the rest of his life in Bergen County, New Jersey (Nixon at his home in Saddle River; and Hoffa, it is rumored, living out his last hours getting fitted for a pair of cement shoes at New Jersey's Meadowlands Sports Complex in East Rutherford, where the New York Giants play).

JIMMY CARTER SETS TRUMAN ASSASSIN FREE!

Twenty-five years after Harry Truman save his own assassin, Oscar Collazo, from execution, Jimmy Carter set him free.

NIXON PARDONS JUST KEEP COMING!

In 1989, Ronald Reagan pardoned George Steinbrenner for making illegal campaign contributions to Richard Nixon's 1972 reelection campaign. Then in 1989, George H. W. Bush pardoned Armand Hammer for making illegal campaign contributions to Richard Nixon's 1972 reelection campaign.

PERHAPS THE PRESIDENT SHOULD PARDON HIMSELF?

EVERYONE KNOWS, OF course, that George Washington refused to accept a salary as president.

But what you may not know is that in lieu of that salary George requested only that his expenses be paid.

Sounds fair, right?

Of course it does, until you realize that Washington had been padding his expense account for years, beginning with his years as chief military officer during the Revolutionary War.

Granted, Washington gave his all for his country, but he also took quite a bit, including lodging and dining for himself, his staff (including a secretary and aide-de-camp), his wife, and their stepson and vast quantities of the best food and wine.

And when George Washington finally submitted his expense report? *He claimed that he had run up a $449,261 tab.*

This is not a "Monica Lewinsky" joke:

One night, long before Monica was even a glint in her father's eye, JFK sent his press secretary Pierre Salinger out to buy a thousand or so of his favorite cigars, which happened to be Upmann Petits from Cuba.

Then the next morning, after Salinger showed up with twelve hundred cigars, Kennedy proceeded to sign an order banning any future Cuban imports into the United States.

MY BROTHER, HE'S DAMN HEAVY

THE NEXT FEW pages are inspired by Roger Clinton, the cocaine-snorting, drug-dealing, drunk-driving, white-trash brother of Bill Clinton, and also by Billy Carter, the beer-guzzling, jaw-flapping, Libyan-lobbyist-bribe-taking, redneck brother of Jimmy Carter.

Meanwhile, it would be a shame not to also mention:

SETTING THE STANDARD FOR FUTURE CIVIL-SERVICE EMPLOYEES

- James Monroe's brother, Joseph, was such a ne'er-do-well with three ex-wives and a mountain of debt that the president hired him as secretary just so he could keep an eye on him and prevent him from getting into any more trouble. (James Monroe also hired his wife's nephew, Samuel Gouverneur, for the same reason.)
- Ulysses S. Grant's brother Orvil (along with the president's son, Frederick Dent Grant) were reportedly implicated in the "Whiskey Ring" scandal, where IRS agents collaborated with liquor distillers to fake production reports and therefore avoid paying taxes; of course, a percentage of the money that was saved from paying taxes was skimmed off and paid to the corrupt IRS agents and others like Grant's son and brother.

276

> Presidents are always having family problems, just like the rest of us. Who doesn't have a relative he would just as soon forget? There's a Roger Clinton or a Billy Carter swinging from every family tree.
>
> —ABC News reporter Buck Wolf

> { "I think I helped Jimmy as much as I hurt him . . . but I certainly didn't hurt him enough to [cause him to] lose 44 states." }
>
> —Billy Carter

- Ulysses S. Grant's brother-in-law Abel Corbin (who was married to Grant's sister Virginia) was part of a scheme to buy gold and then to trick the president into manipulating the price of gold so it would go up sharply in price.
- Richard Nixon's brother, Donald, dreamed of becoming a "Burger King" of sorts by opening his own chain of hamburger joints, but President Nixon was so unnerved by all his brother's get-rich schemes that he ordered the Secret Service to wiretap his brother's phone to make sure he wasn't about to do anything that would be embarrassing during the 1972 Nixon reelection campaign.
- While JFK was president, his brother Teddy confessed to cheating on his law school exams.

How much trouble was Roger Clinton?

Let's put it this way . . . his Secret Service codename was "Headache."

LBJ MADE A PLACE FOR HIS BROTHER SAM AT THE WHITE HOUSE, OF COURSE. . . .

B UT NOT BECAUSE he was fond of Sam, or because Sam had a special job to do for the president.

Rather, it was President Johnson's way of keeping an eye on his brother because Sam was, by his own admission, a "problem drinker," and apparently, Sam had another problem: every time he knocked back a few "adult beverages," he'd start divulging very sensitive and damaging information to the press.

Sam was such a problem for President Johnson that LBJ gave him a home in the White House and had security personnel keep track of him 24/7.

But in his memoirs, Sam Johnson described himself as a prisoner in the White House, unable to step outside without a swarm of Secret Service agents monitoring everything that he did.

PREZ MAKES PITCH FOR HALF BRO'S BIZ

IMAGINE OWNING YOUR own business.

And imagine having a half brother who was the president of the United States.

And now imagine that your half brother makes personal appearances at your business to help you attract more customers.

That'd be pretty nice, right?

Well, that's exactly what President William Howard Taft did for his half brother, Charles Phelps Taft, when he showed up at the Opening Day game for the Washington Senators baseball team on April 14, 1910.

As it turns out, the Senators were playing the Philadelphia Athletics that day, and President Taft's half brother was part owner of the Philly team.

The chance to see the president toss out the first pitch drew quite a few extra fans to the game. (Which was a bit surprising, since Taft was a *very* unpopular president; in fact, he was actually booed and hissed by some as he took to the field.)

How one sports reporter called the Taft pitch: "He did it with his good, trusty right arm, and the virgin sphere scudded across the diamond, true as a die to the pitcher's box, where Walter Johnson gathered it in."

EXECUTIVE PRIVILEGE(S)!

NEIL BUSH: PROBLEM BROTHER, PROBLEM SON

Somehow, whenever we think of presidential brother/presidential son Neil Bush, this scene from the movie *Chinatown* always pops into our heads:

> **Evelyn Mulwray:** She's my daughter.
> [Gittes slaps Evelyn]
> **Jake Gittes:** I said I want the truth!
> **Evelyn Mulwray:** She's my sister . . .
> [slap]
> **Evelyn Mulwray:** She's my daughter . . .
> [slap]
> **Evelyn Mulwray:** My sister, my daughter.
> [More slaps]
> **Jake Gittes:** I said I want the truth!
> **Evelyn Mulwray:** She's my sister AND my daughter!

Neil, of course, is the Bush brother/son who:

- Was involved in the collapse of the Silverado Savings and Loan and the S&L crisis.
- Was cochairman of a company called Crest Investment, which paid him $60,000 per year for "answering phone calls when Jamal Daniel, the other cochairman, called and asked for advice."
- Was paid $2 million in company stock and $10,000 for every board meeting he attended for a Chinese semiconductor company. But, of course, we'd be negligent if we didn't point out that Neil Bush didn't know anything about semiconductors when he took the job.
- Has used his family name and connections to meet with Arab princes, have a private dinner with the president of China, and to negotiate a deal that paid him $642,500 to introduce an Asian investor to a U.S. high-tech company.

Finally, as you read on, you will see there was a "very unusual" thing that just kept happening every time Neil visited the Far East.

EXECUTIVE PRIVILEGE(S)!

WHEN OPPORTUNITY KNOCKS FOR NEIL BUSH, HE ALWAYS OPENS THE DOOR!

"Mr. Bush, you have to admit it's a pretty remarkable thing for a man just to go to a hotel room door and open it and have a woman standing there and have sex with her. . . ."

—Marshall Davis Brown, divorce attorney repre-senting Sharon Bush duing a deposition of Neil Bush

"It was VERY unusual. . . ."

—Neil Bush's response

While getting divorced from his wife Sharon, Neil disclosed in a deposition with Sharon's attorney that during repeated business trips in the late 1990s, he had sex with strange women who just happened to show up at his door at various hotels in Hong Kong and Thailand.

Neil, of course, claimed that he didn't know a thing about these women—whether or not they were prostitutes, what made them decide to knock at his door, who sent them to his door—because he didn't ask.

He just welcomed them into his room and had sex with them . . . and that was that.

PLEASE DO AS I SAY . . .
NOT AS I TAUGHT MY CHILDREN TO DO

Robert Johnson, son of President Andrew Johnson, illustrates an important lesson in life for us all:

If you're the son of the president, it's a bad idea to pick up a prostitute and take her back to your place. Especially when you actually live at the White House in addition to working there for your dad!

We like to call it "The (Margarita) Shot Heard 'Round the World!":

Underage twins Jenna and Barbara Bush. A night of drinking. A couple of fake IDs. Need we say more?

"Have you been drinking, Son?"

In the case of John Tyler's son, John, the answer was obviously "Yes." And the drinking got to be such a problem that Tyler eventually had to fire John, who also happened to be his press secretary!

Alice Roosevelt, Holy Terror:

Much can be said about Teddy Roosevelt's oldest child, Alice.

- When her parents told her she could not smoke under their roof, she took her cigarettes up to the White House roof.
- When other women found it fashionable to wear feather boas, Alice decided to wear a REAL boa to an event.
- After she took a real dislike to William Howard Taft's wife, Alice buried a voodoo doll in the front yard of the White House as a way to put a curse onto Taft and his wife.

Chester Alan Arthur's skinny-dipping son Alan:

He got caught swimming nude in the White House's South Lawn fountain in the middle of the night . . . along with the Prince of Siam.

EXECUTIVE PRIVILEGE(S)!

My God, this is a hell of a job! I have no trouble with my enemies. I can take care of my enemies all right. But my damn friends, my g-damn friends . . . they're the ones that keep me walking the floor nights!

— President Warren Harding, after he realized the downside of having extended the rights of executive privilege to his no-good friends

THE PROBLEM WITH
THE "WARREN" COMMISSION:

Aren't you glad you do a better job of choosing your friends than Warren Harding did?

- Charles Forbes was Harding's head of the Veteran's Bureau . . . and he was also caught defrauding the government of $200 million by taking kickbacks when buying goods, skimming profits when selling goods, and even selling bootlegged drugs to drug dealers.
- Forbes's assistant was Charles Cramer . . . and he shot himself to death. Why? No one knows. Even though he left a suicide note behind addressed to Harding, Harding never read it.
- Harry Daugherty was Harding's attorney general . . . and he was also caught selling alcohol during Prohibition.
- Daugherty's assistant was Jess Smith . . . and he killed himself, too.
- Albert Fall was Harding's secretary of the interior . . . and he got caught taking more than $400,000 in kickbacks and loans while leasing to oil companies the oil rights in Wyoming's Teapot Dome and California's Elk Hills reserves. Fall eventually spent a year in jail and was fined $100,000 for being the mastermind behind the "Teapot Dome" scandal.

"If you were
a girl, Warren,
you'd be in the
family way all the time.
You can't say no."

—Warren Harding's
father, George

EXECUTIVE PRIVILEGE(S)!

"When I came into power, I found that the party managers had taken it all to themselves. I could not name my own Cabinet. They had sold out every place to pay the election expenses."

— President Benjamin Harrison

"A man who has never gone to school may steal from a freight train; but if he has a university education, he may steal the whole railroad."

—-President Theodore Roosevelt

THE PRESIDENTIAL "FRIEND" FACTOR

A T FIRST, YOU might think that being a friend of the president would be a really great thing that included lots of perks, like:

Personal White House Tours!

Invitations to fancy-schmanzy dinners!!

Wonderful opportunities to get really cushy government jobs!!!

And to be fair, we think the first two items above are every president's right to share with friends. In fact, if one of us is ever elected president, we'll do the same.

But that third item, let's face it: it's a loaded public-relations gun for every president. Just ask Harriet Miers.

She was President George W. Bush's White House counsel and his former personal attorney. And even though she had absolutely no judicial experience and no experience with constitutional law, he thought he'd nominate her to the Supreme Court anyway.

Now, to be fair to President Bush, some Americans and members of Congress agreed with him when he said that he thought her lack of experience as a judge would bring a "fresh perspective" to the bench. But clearly, not enough Americans or members of Congress (or members of the press!) went along, and Miers withdrew her nomination as a nominee for the Supreme Court a few weeks later.

Of course, this isn't the first time a president has offered a friend (or friends) a peach of a government job only to see those job offerings blow up in his face.

EXECUTIVE PRIVILEGE(S)!

MY FRIEND, MY PRESIDENT, MY MEAL-TICKET

Look, here's the problem: If you're the president, you've got to surround yourself with your "people." You know: cabinet members, aides, advisors, staffers. And when it comes to filling these jobs, who are you going to think of first? People you know, of course. People you know and trust.

Is that cronyism? Or nepotism?

No, it's not—if those people are truly qualified for the job you're offering. And yes, it is—if they're not.

So the hard part, when you're president, is asking yourself:

"How do I figure out who *is* qualified? And how do I let down gently those friends and family who *think* they're qualified for lofty government positions, but they're really *not*?"

You'd think this would be pretty easy stuff for someone smart enough to be elected Leader of the Free World, but as you will see, history sometimes shows that this is one of the hardest parts of the job.

CRONYISM = SCANDALISM???

As you may recall, in our earlier "Money!" chapter, we pointed out that the three presidents with the most corrupt administrations were Buchanan, Grant, and Truman.

Why?

Well, in Buchanan's case, his administration was corrupt because he himself was corrupt.

But in the case of Grant and Truman, both were very honest guys; it was their amazing loyalty to old friends that brought corruption (and tons of it!) into their administrations.

ULYSSES S. GRANT AND THE "FRIEND FACTOR"

- Grant's vice president, Schuyler Colfax, resigned after it was discovered that he had taken bribes earlier in his political career.
- Grant's secretary of war, William Belknap, resigned after it was found that both his first and second wives (and they were sisters!) had taken bribes, and that he, too, had personally received kickbacks from time to time.
- Grant's secretary of the navy, George Robeson, resigned after it was discovered that he had received $300,000 in kickbacks for handing out defense contracts to friends.
- Grant's ambassador to Brazil, James Watson Webb, got caught taking a $100,000 bribe from the Brazilian government.
- Grant's assistant treasurer, General Daniel Butterfield, admitted to being a part of the "black Friday" gold panic and also admitted to committing perjury.
- Grant appointed his friend General John D. McDonald as head of the IRS, and McDonald was later implicated in the "Whiskey Ring" scandal that involved IRS agents falsifying reports and keeping some liquor taxes for themselves.
- Grant's personal secretary, Orville E. Babcock, and other friends were also implicated in the "Whiskey Ring" scandal.

289

EXECUTIVE PRIVILEGE(S)!

HARRY TRUMAN AND THE "FRIEND FACTOR"

- Truman made an old buddy from the Missouri National Guard, his former tea-salesman friend Harry Vaughn, coordinator of Veteran Affairs. Vaughn is most famous for hinting to a lobbyist that he and the president both needed new freezers at their homes, so the manufacturer sent free freezers to Harry Truman's house back in Missouri, to Harry Vaughn, and to four other well-placed Truman friends in the administration, and a huge scandal about the gifts erupted.

- Truman's presidential appointments secretary, Matthew Connelly, was found guilty of accepting all kinds of gifts—cash, one of Harry Vaughn's freezers, suits and other clothing, and even oil royalties. In the end, he did time for bribery, perjury, and conspiracy.

- Truman's personal physician, Dr. Wallace Graham, was investigated by a Senate subcommittee for fraud and corruption, and he admitted to engaging in insider trading.

- A variety of Truman friends (and friends of Truman friends) were implicated in shady dealings with the "Reconstruction Finance Corporation," which was created during the Hoover presidency to give financial assistance to bankrupt companies during the Depression. Among the Truman friends who were accused of wrongdoings:

  - Personnel executive Donald Dawson was investigated by Congress and found guilty of a variety of financial improprieties.
  - RFC examiner E. Merl Young made a loan to one company, then went to work for the same company the day after the loan was approved; he also got on the payroll of other companies after he got their RFC loans approved. Young also took as a bribe a mink coat for his wife, which later led to Richard Nixon's reference to his wife's "respectable, Republican cloth coat" during his infamous televised "Checkers" speech while running for vice president under Eisenhower.
  - While on the White House payroll, attorney William Boyle took kickbacks for helping companies get RFC loans.

290

And sometimes, friends of presidents give up a lot, too:

"My holdings [in General Motors] may sound like a lot,
[but] as a percentage of General Motors they are
less than one-tenth of one percent."

—General Motors CEO "Engine" Charlie Wilson*,
after he was told he would have to give up his $600,000/year salary
and sell his $2.5 million in GM stock before he could become
Eisenhower's secretary of defense

*He was called "Engine" Charlie so he wouldn't be confused with "Electric" Charlie, the "other" Charles Wilson, who was head of General Electric and the Office of Defense Mobilization for Harry Truman.

EXECUTIVE PRIVILEGE(S)!

12
Take This Job and Shove It!

M<small>Y</small> G<small>OD</small>! W<small>HAT</small> is there in this place [the White House] that a man should ever want to get into it?" James Garfield once asked.

Hey, it's a mystery to us, too.

And before you assume Garfield was just suffering from a bad attitude problem or start asking yourself, *How bad could it really be?* you should consider this: Garfield couldn't have been in office for very long before he came to this conclusion about what a horrible job the presidency was, because less than four months after he was inaugurated someone shot him in the back.

"AND YOU CAN QUOTE ME ON THAT!"

George Washington

"My movements to the chair of government will be accompanied by feelings not unlike those of a culprit who is going to the place of his execution."

John Adams

"No man who ever held the office of president would congratulate a friend on obtaining it. He will make one man ungrateful, and a hundred men his enemies, for every office he can bestow."

"If I were to go over my life again, I would be a shoemaker rather than an American statesman."

Or was it George's smile they were admiring?

After his inauguration, John Adams commented to his wife that it really irked him that instead of looking at him, everyone in the crowd had their admiring eyes locked on Washington. He seemed to "enjoy a triumph over me," Adams told his wife. "Me thought I heard him say, 'Ay, I am fairly out and you fairly in! See which of us will be happiest.'"

Thomas Jefferson

"Politics is such a torment that I would advise everyone I love not to mix with it."

"To myself personally, it brings nothing but unceasing drudgery and daily loss of friends."

"I have the consolation . . . of having added nothing to my private fortune during my public service, and of retiring with hands as clean as they are empty."

(Jefferson died nearly penniless at the age of eighty-three.)

John Quincy Adams

"The four most miserable years of my life were my four years in the presidency."

Andrew Jackson

"I can say with truth that mine is a situation of dignified slavery."

Martin Van Buren

"As to the presidency, the two happiest days of my life were those of my entrance upon the office and my surrender of it."

James Polk

"The office of president is generally esteemed a very high and dignified position. . . . I think the public would not so regard it if they could . . . observe the kind of people by whom I am often annoyed."

James Buchanan (to newly elected President Abraham Lincoln)

"If you are as happy, my dear sir, on entering the White House as I in leaving it and returning home, you are the happiest man in the country."

TAKE THIS JOB AND SHOVE IT!

Abraham Lincoln

"From my boyhood up, it was my ambition to be president. Now I am president of one part of this divided country, at least; but look at me! I wish I had never been born!"

"I am like the man who was tarred and feathered and ridden out of town on a rail. When they asked him how he felt about it, he said that if it were not for the honor of the thing, he would rather have walked."

Rutherford B. Hayes

"My day is frittered away by the personal seeking of people, when I ought to be given to the great problems which concern the whole country. Four years of this kind of intellectual dissipation may cripple me for the remainder of my life."

"Being an errand boy to one hundred and fifty thousand people tires me so by night I am ready for bed instead of soirees."

Grover Cleveland

"The office of president has not, to me personally, a single allurement."

(Still, after he lost a bid for reelection in 1888, he ran again in 1892 and won, making him the only president to serve nonconsecutive terms.)

Theodore Roosevelt (in a note to his friend and successor, William Howard Taft)

"Ha ha! You are making up your Cabinet. I in a lighthearted way have spent the morning testing the rifles for my African trip."

William Howard Taft

"I have come to the conclusion that the major part of the work of a president is to increase the gate receipts of expositions and fairs and bring the tourists into the town."

"I am glad to be going. This is the lonesomest place in the world."

(as he left the White House the final time)

Warren G. Harding

"My God, this is a hell of a place for a man like me to be!"

"The White House is a prison. I can't get away from the men who dog my footsteps. I am in jail."

Herbert Hoover

"This job is nothing but a twenty-ring circus—with a whole lot of bad actors."

"All the money in the world could not induce me to live over the last nine months. The conditions we have experienced make this office a compound hell."

Dwight Eisenhower

Unlike most of his fellow presidents, Ike didn't really want the job and was complaining about it even before it was his:

"I furiously object to the word 'candidate'—I ain't and won't."

"I don't know why people are always nagging me to run for president. I think I've gotten too old."

TAKE THIS JOB AND SHOVE IT!

"Those fools on the National Committee! Are they trying to perform the feat of electing a dead man?"

"I cannot conceive of any circumstance that could drag out of me permission to consider me for any political post from dogcatcher to Grand High Supreme King of the Universe."

"In the strongest language you can command you can state that I have no political ambitions at all. Make it even stronger than that if you can."

Once he had the job, Ike's chief complaint was that he could never get in a game of golf without being interrupted with phone calls from the State Department.

AND THE ONE THAT GOT AWAY . . .

"I will not accept if nominated and will not serve if elected. . . . If forced to choose between the penitentiary and the White House for four years . . . I would say the penitentiary, thank you."

—Civil War general William Tecumseh Sherman in 1884

WHITE HOUSE: CONFIDENTIAL

CONCLUSION

WHEN YOU WRITE for a living you're constantly asked, "What are you working on?" And when asked that question during the writing of this book, we would always describe it in short detail. Almost uniformly, the response to our description would be one echoing a constant sentiment: that the men we elect as presidents today don't come close to measuring up to the standards of our forefathers. Conventional wisdom tells us, it seems, that our political ancestors were smarter, more honest, and more gentlemanly than politicians today.

We were always delighted to hear this response because it perfectly expressed what had been our anti-premise for the book since its date of conception.

In fact, this comment, which we heard over and over again, reminded us of a not particularly profound, but still very interesting, phenomenon of human nature: Members of a younger generation will very often assume members of older generations were boring and well-behaved when they were at a similar age. One result of this misperception is that it always leads each successive generation to assume the sins and crimes and scandals of the present day are the worst the world has ever known. But hopefully, now that you've read this far, you've begun to look at history (at least as it pertains to our presidents) in a different light.

If you think about it, long before Watergate, Contragate, Travelgate, Nannygate, and Paulagate, our presidents were lying, cheating, stealing, and womanizing—so the idea that our current crop of presidents don't "measure up" is both an inaccurate and a silly one. We don't mean to say George Bush is a modern-day George Washington and Bill Clinton is a modern-day Thomas Jefferson. Rather, our point is that, of the forty-one men who have served as president of the United States, only Washington, Jefferson, Lincoln, Roosevelt, Roosevelt, and Truman have been of the caliber of Washington, Jefferson, Lincoln, Roosevelt, Roosevelt, and Truman. The rest have been (dare we say it?) mostly Fillmores,

Pierces, Johnsons, Arthurs, and Clevelands. In other words: pretty darn average, pretty darn modest in the brains and talent departments, and . . . pretty darn forgettable.

Given the qualifiers above, what kind of feat is it to "measure up" to the standards of our forefathers anyway? Surely our current president and his last few predecessors have been at least as average and forgettable as most of the presidents of our past.

Which brings us to our true premise.

We began this book by suggesting that perhaps presidents ought not be judged by their ability to govern or lead but by their ability to entertain—which is an interesting concept since the number and severity of a president's imbroglios seem to have nothing to do with his ability to govern and lead.

History will always remember Buchanan and Harding, for instance, as scandalous guys who made terrible presidents. In contrast, Jefferson and FDR will always be remembered as great presidents . . . who just happened to be scandalous as well.

And how will history remember Madison? McKinley? Harrison? Harrison? Or Hayes? The answer is history will barely remember them at all. These men were boring in life and boring in office—they failed to entertain. And when you've been elected to the office of president of the United States, there is no greater sign of failure and no worse slap in the face than to be remembered as a guy who did nothing that was worth being remembered for . . . or to get all the way to the White House but not be remembered at all.

With all this in mind, we offer you this quote a president once made to a friend about his predecessor: "If he was not the greatest president, he was the best actor of presidency we have ever had."

If we asked you to guess which president was being described, you'd be hard-pressed not to pick Ronald Reagan, of course.

But you'd be wrong.

The speaker was John Adams. And the president he was describing was none other than George Washington.

And that, dear reader, is entertainment.

It's impossible for us to draw this book to a close without saying something about media bias.

Trying to unravel the relationship between the presidency and the media (and you, the recipient of their final product) is sort of like trying to unravel the relationship between the chicken, the egg, and Einstein's theory of relativity. It would be fun to figure out which came first, the chicken or the egg, but as Einstein's theory demonstrates, "first" is a matter of one's point of view.

Interestingly, news and politics work in a similar way. Case in point: Gregg once had a conversation with the very conservative Oliver North in which North explained that he got a lot of his news from CNN even though he felt the network added a "left-wing" slant to their reporting. Not long afterward, Gregg had a conversation with the very liberal Frank Zappa, who explained why he didn't like to watch too much CNN: "I find that their presentation is slanted and . . . so Republican, it's just smelly and it's suspicious."

So, which is it—the chicken or the egg? As Einstein might say, it all depends on your perspective.

Regardless of which direction you like to see your news slant, any attempts to view the contents of this book as an attack on (or a vote in support of) one particular political party or another will only be misguided. When it comes to presidential peccadilloes, we just called 'em as we saw 'em, and in true bipartisan spirit, we did it without paying any attention to party lines.

Gregg Stebben
San Francisco, California
July 2006

Austin Hill
Phoenix, Arizona
July 2006

CONCLUSION

APPENDIX A: WHAT'S IN A NAME?

WELL, IF YOU consider that in 1958 a guy named John F. Kennedy, who worked in the stockroom of a razor factory, ran for the office of treasurer of Massachusetts and won on the strength of his name alone, you might begin to think there's more in a name than you presumed—especially if your name happens to be the same as Senator John Fitzgerald Kennedy's.

There's more than a little irony in this story, given that JFK's dad did essentially the same thing to help JFK get elected the first time he ran for office.

The year was 1946, and Kennedy was running for Congress. Joe Sr. was worried that a popular Boston city councilman, Joseph Russo, would get the upper hand in the race, so he cleverly went out and found another Joe Russo and paid him to put his name on the ballot.

In the end the two Joes split the Russo vote, and JFK won the election.

By the way, the JFK name not only bought the second Mr. Kennedy the election, it also allowed him to do it dirt cheap. In fact, his total campaign expenses amounted to about one hundred dollars—most of which was spent to throw an election-night party.

Gerald Ford:	When Gerald Ford was born he was given the name Leslie Lynch King, but when his father died and his mother remarried, he was given his adoptive father's name: Gerald Ford. Therefore, punsters like to point out, Gerald Ford is the only president "born a King."
John F. Kennedy:	JFK called his daughter, Caroline, "Buttons," and she called him "Silly Daddy." JFK called John Jr. "Foo Foo Head."
Harry Truman:	Harry Truman called his wife, Bess, "The Boss" and his daughter, Margaret, "the one who bosses 'The Boss.'" The Secret Service called Truman, his wife, and his daughter "The Three Musketeers."

APPENDIX A: WHAT'S IN A NAME?

"I was supposed to be named Harrison Shippe Truman, taking the middle name from my paternal grandfather. Others in the family wanted my middle name to be Solomon, taken from my maternal grandfather. But apparently no agreement could be reached and my name was recorded and stands simply as Harry S Truman."

—Harry Truman

(Note the absence of a period after his middle initial; since it doesn't stand for anything it's technically not an initial and therefore does not require traditional punctuation.)

Woodrow Wilson:	Folk singer Woodie Guthrie was named after Woodrow Wilson; his real name was Woodrow Wilson Guthrie.
Abe Lincoln:	Lincoln Logs were, in fact, named after Abraham Lincoln and the log cabin where Abe was born. Interestingly, Lincoln Logs were invented by John Lloyd Wright, the son of the famous architect Frank Lloyd Wright.
William Henry Harrison:	Boxer Jack Dempsey was named after President William Henry Harrison, believe it or not. Dempsey's real name was William Harrison Dempsey.
James Monroe:	The capital of the nation of Liberia is called Monrovia in honor of President James Monroe.
Richard Nixon:	Everyone's got a namesake, and Richard Nixon's was King Richard the Lion-Hearted.
LBJ:	It took good planning on the part of the Johnson family to get every member to have the same LBJ initials: Lyndon Baines, Lady Bird, Lynda Bird, and Luci Baines. As LBJ told it, when it came to monogramming, it made things a whole lot cheaper.
Andrew Jackson:	Andrew Jackson Borden, a mortician from Fall River, Massachusetts, had the honor of being named after the seventh president. But he is more famous for being murdered by his youngest daughter, Lizzie.

APPENDIX A: WHAT'S IN A NAME?

APPENDIX B: PRESIDENTIAL FIRSTS

YOU KNOW, IMPORTANT stuff like which president was the first to wear a ponytail and which was the first to go snowboarding:

President: **George Washington**

Years in office: 1789–1797

Political first: George Washington became the first president to use a speechwriter when he asked Thomas Jefferson, James Madison, and Alexander Hamilton to help him draft his farewell address.

President: **John Adams**

Years in office: 1797–1801

Political first: John Adams was the first to serve as president and then lose in a reelection bid.

Social first: John Adams and his family were the first to live in the White House. When it was time for the entire federal government to move its temporary quarters in Philadelphia to the new capitol in Washington D.C. the entire enterprise—every document and file—fit into just seven packing cases.

President: **Thomas Jefferson**

Years in office: 1801–1809

Political first: Thomas Jefferson was subpoenaed to testify in the treason trial of Aaron Burr, and he became the first president to invoke executive privilege.

Social first: Thomas Jefferson was the first president to do away with bowing and to offer his hand for a handshake instead.

President:	**James Madison**
Years in office:	1809–1817
Political first:	James Madison is the only president to have led troops into battle while he was in office. He did so while the British were trying to invade Washington during the War of 1812.
Social first:	James Madison was the first president to wear trousers, while his successor, James Monroe, was the last president to wear knee breeches, buckled shoes, and three-cornered hats. Interestingly, Madison tended to push for change in government policy, while Monroe generally liked to keep things status quo.

President:	**John Quincy Adams**
Years in office:	1825–1829
Technological first:	John Quincy Adams was the first president to ride on a train and the first to be photographed.

President:	**Andrew Jackson**
Years in office:	1829–1837
Political firsts:	He was the first president to be born in a log cabin.
	He was the first president to have an assassination attempt made on his life.
	He is thought to be our "dueling-est" president ever.

President:	**Martin Van Buren**
Years in office:	1837–1841
Social first:	Martin Van Buren was the first president to be born after the Declaration of Independence was signed and the first to be a United States citizen (all previous presidents were born British subjects).

President:	**William Henry Harrison**
Years in office:	1841–1841
Social first:	Not only was William Henry Harrison the first to die in office, but he also was the fastest to die—only thirty-one days after taking office.

President:	**John Tyler**
Years in office:	1841–1845
Political firsts:	Since President Harrison died after only thirty-one days in office, Tyler served the shortest term of any vice president.
	When William Henry Harrison died, John Tyler became the first VP to succeed to the office of president.
	He was the first to have a presidential veto overruled by Congress.

President:	**Zachary Taylor**
Years in office:	1849–1850
Political first:	Zachary Taylor was the first elected president who had never held a public office before. In fact, he had never even voted before—and he didn't even vote for himself.

President:	**Franklin Pierce**
Years in office:	1853–1857
Social first:	Franklin Pierce was the first president to have a Christmas tree in the White House.

APPENDIX B: PRESIDENTIAL FIRSTS

President:	**James Buchanan**
Years in office:	1857–1861
Technological first:	James Buchanan was the first president ever to send or receive a transatlantic telegram.
Social first:	On the grand occasion of that first telegram, he exchanged greetings with the queen of England.

President:	**Abraham Lincoln**
Years in office:	1861–1865
Technological first:	Abe is the only president ever to receive a patent—#6469. His invention? A very complex device that used chambers of air to allow heavy ships to pass over shallow and dangerous waters.
Social firsts:	Abraham Lincoln was the first president to have a beard. As the story goes, he was clean-shaven when he was nominated but decided to grow a beard after he got a letter from a little girl named Grace Bedell who wrote [sic]:

> I have got 4 brothers and part of them will vote for you any way
> and if you let your whiskers grow I will try and get the rest of them
> to vote for you. You would look a great deal better for your face is
> so thin. All the ladies like whiskers and they would tease their hus-
> band's to vote for you and then you would be president.

Lincoln did as she suggested and then stopped his campaign train when it passed through her hometown. When Grace and her family joined the crowd assembled around Lincoln, he called her up to the front, kissed her, and said, "You see, I let these whiskers grow for you, Grace."

The first child to die in the White House was Abraham Lincoln's twelve-year-old son, Willie.

POLITICAL FIRST: WAS CHET ARTHUR
THE FIRST CANADIAN U.S. PRESIDENT???

OR NO PRESIDENT AT ALL?

Most history books count Chester A. Arthur as the twenty-first president of the United States, first elected vice president under James Garfield, then succeeding to the presidency when Garfield was assassinated.

But we'd like to suggest that perhaps Chester A. Arthur was never president at all. Why? Because Chet's dad was a Baptist minister from Vermont, and he preached on both sides of the U.S.–Canada border, and some historians believe that Chet Arthur was actually born in Canada but later assumed the identity of a stillborn brother who was born in the United States so he could enjoy the benefits of U.S. citizenship.

This may help explain why some sources report that Chester A. Arthur was born in 1829, while others report that he was born in 1830. Or as one book, *U.S. Presidents Factbook,* explains it: "Arthur's birth date is often given as 1830, but this is incorrect—Arthur made himself a year younger when he was in his forties."

Weird? Yes.

But you've got to figure that any man who thinks he has the power to make himself a year younger would also assume he had the power to change himself from a Canadian into a U.S. citizen, right?

President: **Rutherford B. Hayes**

Years in office: 1877–1881

Technological first: Rutherford B. Hayes was the first president to have a typewriter. He also had the first telephone installed in the White House.

President: **Chester Alan Arthur**

Years in office: 1881–1885

Social first: Chester A. Arthur was the first president to smoke cigarettes.

President: **Grover Cleveland**

Years in office: 1885–1889, 1893–1897

Social first: Grover Cleveland was the first and only president to get married in the White House.

President: **Benjamin Harrison**

Years in office: 1889–1893

Technological first: Benjamin Harrison was the first president to have electricity in the White House.

President: **William McKinley**

Years in office: 1897–1901

Technological first: William McKinley was the first to use the telephone as part of his campaign strategy and the first to ride in a self-propelled vehicle—the electric ambulance that took him to the hospital after he had been shot.

President:	**Teddy Roosevelt**
Years in office:	1901–1909
Political firsts:	Teddy Roosevelt was the first vice president to succeed to the presidency and then win the office in an election on his own. He was also the youngest man ever to serve as president—when McKinley died—although JFK was the youngest man ever elected.
	When Teddy Roosevelt made a trip to Panama to check on progress of the Panama Canal, it was the first time a president had ever left the country while in office.
	The first Jewish cabinet member, Oscar Straus, was appointed by Teddy Roosevelt. He was the head of the newly formed Department of Commerce and Labor.
Technological first:	Teddy Roosevelt was the first president to ride in a car, go underwater in a submarine, and fly in a plane, although the plane trip was after he left office. His sub ride was in the *U.S.S. Plunger* and lasted about an hour. His airplane trip was at the St. Louis Aviation Field in a plane built by the Wright brothers. During the course of the trip, which lasted four minutes, the average cruising altitude was fifty feet.

{ In spite of the fact that TR was the first president to experience advanced modes of transportation, he once blew up at his twenty-two-year-old daughter, Alice, and shouted, "The Roosevelts will remain a horse family!" when she suggested she'd like to travel by car once in a while. }

APPENDIX B: PRESIDENTIAL FIRSTS

Social firsts:	TR was the first to invite an African American to the White House for dinner. His guest was botanist Booker T. Washington.
	He was the first president to win the Nobel Peace Prize. (The only other presidents to win were Woodrow Wilson and Jimmy Carter.)

President:	**William H. Taft**
Years in office:	1909–1913
Political firsts:	William H. Taft was the first president required to pay federal income tax on his presidential salary.
	He is the only president to have served on the Supreme Court; he was eventually named chief justice.
Social first:	He was the first president to start the baseball season by throwing out the first pitch. Call it nepotism: After all, his brother was part owner of the Philadelphia Athletics. (It is also rumored that Taft is responsible for the seventh-inning stretch, which grew out of an incident where he tried to get out of his seat and his three-hundred-plus-pound frame got stuck.)

314

President:	**Woodrow Wilson**
Years in office:	1913–1921
Technological firsts:	Wilson was the last president to ride to his inauguration in a horse-drawn carriage.
	He was also the first to cross the Atlantic.
Social first:	Woodrow Wilson was the first president to show a motion picture at the White House. Interestingly, the film was *Birth of a Nation,* which is considered by many film scholars to be one of the most important films in history because of its many technical innovations. (For instance, it was the first film to use night photography, tinting for dramatic effect, and close-up shots to reveal the intimate thoughts of a character.) On the other hand, because of its explicit and positive portrayal of the Ku Klux Klan, it is also the most banned film in American history.

President:	**Warren G. Harding**
Years in office:	1921–1923
Technological first:	Warren G. Harding was the first president to own a radio and the first to make a speech over the radio waves. He was also the first to ride to his inauguration in a car and the first to know how to drive.
Social first:	When women got the right to vote, Harding was the first president they could elect.

President:	**FDR**
Years in office:	1933–1945
Political firsts:	The first woman to serve on a president's cabinet was Frances Perkins, appointed by FDR to the position of secretary of labor. She was once asked if she thought being a woman was in any way a handicap. "Only in climbing trees," she replied.
	Not only was FDR the first president to be elected for more than two terms (the tradition of seeking no more than two terms was unofficial, based on the precedence set by George Washington), but he was also the first candidate ever to win a presidential nomination after losing a bid for the vice presidency.
Technological firsts:	Using a special switch that was set up at the White House, FDR was able to turn on the lights at Crosby Field in Cincinnati for the first night game in major league baseball history. (The Reds beat the Phillies 4-1.)
	The first bomb shelter and the first dishwasher were both installed in the White House during FDR's term in office.
	FDR was the first president ever to appear on television and the first president to fly in an airplane while in office (Teddy Roosevelt flew earlier, but not while in office).

APPENDIX B: PRESIDENTIAL FIRSTS

President:	**Harry Truman**
Years in office:	1945–1953
Political first:	In 1948, sixty-four-year-old Harry Truman and seventy-year-old Alben Barkley were the oldest president-vice president team in history. Despite his age, Barkley campaigned in twenty-six states, delivering as many as fifteen speeches a day.

President:	**Dwight D. Eisenhower**
Years in office:	1953–1961
Technological firsts:	Dwight Eisenhower was the first president to appear on color TV.
	He was also the first president to go underwater in an atomic sub.
	He was the first president to have a pilot's license, and it was he who first used helicopters when making short trips on official business.
Social first:	Ike was the first president to hit a hole in one.

President:	**JFK**
Years in office:	1961–1963
Political first:	JFK won the presidency by a mere 120,000 votes out of a total of sixty-nine million ballots cast—the smallest margin ever. (This statistic actually tells only part of the story because it includes the votes cast for all minor-party candidates, as well as his Republican opponent, Richard Nixon. The number of votes that separated him from Nixon tells the true story: JFK did not win the votes of the majority of voters and could only claim one-tenth of 1 percent more popular votes than Nixon.
Social firsts:	JFK was the first Roman Catholic to be president. His one problem? It was difficult for him to find a priest to whom he could confess without the priest recognizing his voice.
	JFK was the first Boy Scout ever to become president.
	He was the first president to be born in the twentieth century.

President:	**LBJ**
Years in office:	1963–1969
Political firsts:	LBJ appointed the first African-American to a cabinet position. His name was Robert C. Weaver, and he was the head of the new Department of Housing and Urban Renewal.
	In the election of 1964, LBJ won 61 percent of the popular vote—more than any other president in history.
	LBJ was the first president to be present at his predecessor's assassination. He was also the first president to have his oath administered by a woman, the first to take his oath in an airplane, and the first to take the oath as his wife held the Bible. (His first presidential order after taking the oath was "Now, let's get airborne.")
Technological first:	While in Australia, Johnson decided to fly back to Washington via Europe instead of over the Pacific, as he had come . . . and by doing so became the first president to circumnavigate the globe.
Social first:	When LBJ went to see the Washington Redskins play the Baltimore Colts in a preseason game in 1966, he became the first president to attend a professional football game while in office.

President:	**Richard Nixon**
Years in office:	1969–1974
Political first:	Richard Nixon is the only person ever elected twice to both the office of vice president and the office of president. He's also the only president ever to resign.
Social first:	Richard Nixon is the only president to have been nominated for a Grammy award; he was nominated in the category of Best Spoken Word album for a recording of a televised interview with David Frost he did after leaving the presidency.

APPENDIX B: PRESIDENTIAL FIRSTS

If you were born in 1953 or 1954, you were the first in the history of the nation to vote at age eighteen . . . and when you went to vote for the first time, you had the choice of Richard Nixon or George McGovern.

President: **Gerald Ford**

Years in office: 1974–1977

Political first: Gerald Ford was the first person to hold the office of vice president—and president—without being elected by the people; he was appointed vice president when Spiro Agnew resigned and then succeeded to the presidency when Nixon resigned.

President: **Jimmy Carter**

Years in office: 1977–1981

Political first: Jimmy Carter appointed the first female African-American cabinet member, Patricia Roberts Harris. She was head of the Department of Housing and Urban Renewal.

Social firsts: Jimmy Carter was the first president born in a hospital.

He is the first known president to go on record as having seen a UFO. The time was 1969, two years before he was elected governor of Georgia. The place: a Lion's Club meeting in Leary, Georgia. Jimmy and ten other club members spotted the object, which Jimmy described as "bright as the moon," "blueish at first, then reddish, luminious, not solid," and seeming to "move toward us from a distance, stop, move partially away, return, then depart." He also reported, in a detailed "sighting report" for the International UFO Bureau in Oklahoma City, that he had watched the

WHITE HOUSE: CONFIDENTIAL

object for ten to twelve minutes, that it produced no sound, and that it appeared to be about nine hundred yards away. "I'll never make fun of people who say they've seen unidentified objects in the sky," he was later heard to say. Jody Powell, Carter's press secretary, once quipped, "I would venture to say he [Carter] probably has seen stranger and more unexplainable things than that during his time in government."

President:	**Ronald Reagan**
Years in office:	1981–1989
Political first:	The first Hispanic cabinet member was Lauro S. Cavazos, who was secretary of education under President Reagan.
Social first:	Ronald Reagan was the first actor ever elected to the presidency, the oldest man ever elected to the office, the first to have been divorced, and the first to suffer from Alzheimer's disease.

President:	**George H. W. Bush**
Years in office:	1989–1993
Technological first:	George Bush was the first to use a personal computer.
Social first:	George Bush was the first president to be asked by the press if he had ever committed adultery.

President:	**Bill Clinton**
Years in office:	1993–2001
Technological first:	Bill Clinton was the first president to have his administration represented on the Internet, although visiting www.billclinton.com at one time would actually link you to the Adult Chamber of Commerce, Eldorado Adult Novelties, Garlic Crabs Delivered Worldwide, and Florida Tile & Marble Installations.

APPENDIX B: PRESIDENTIAL FIRSTS

Social firsts:	He was the first president to be both sued for sexual misconduct and forced to give a deposition while in office.
	He was the first Rhodes scholar ever elected president.
Political first:	He is the first president to be married to a U.S. Senator.
President:	**George W. Bush**
Years in office:	2001 –present
Technological firsts:	He is the first acting president to own an iPod.
	He is the first acting president to use the word "blog" in a speech.
Social first:	He is the first acting president ever to go mountain biking.

Once you go Mac, you'll never go back

"Lightweight, and crank it on, and you shuffle the shuffle
. . . and if you don't like it, you have got your little
advance button. It's pretty high-tech stuff."
—George W. Bush, showing Fox News anchor
Brit Hume how his iPod Shuffle works

APPENDIX C:
THE GEORGE WASHINGTON CONSPIRACY

G EORGE WASHINGTON; FATHER of our country. America's first president. Right?

Wrong.

Do the math. The thirteen original colonies of the United States of America proclaimed their independence in 1776. George Washington became president in 1789. That leaves a gap of thirteen years—thirteen years when someone must have been running the country . . . right?

Right. And that first someone was a guy by the name of John Hanson—who won the job by a unanimous vote of Congress.

Hanson was then followed by Elias Boudinot, the second president of the United States. And Thomas Mifflin, the third president. Richard Henry Lee, the fourth. Nathan Gorman, the fifth. Arthur St. Clair, the sixth. Cyrus Griffin, the seventh. And George Washington, the eighth.

Pretty weird, huh?

IT'S GEORGE WASHINGTON AND THE SEVEN (POLITICAL) DWARVES

If seven different men really did serve as president before George Washington, why did we all learn in school that George was number one?

Because George was the first president to rule under the Constitution we follow today. His seven predecessors, on the other hand, all served as president under the Articles of Confederation, a sort of first-draft Constitution.

Many historians deny the legitimacy of Hanson's presidency because the Articles of Confederation only served to bring the thirteen colonies together into a sort of loose association or "league of friendship" called the Continental Congress.

According to the Articles of Confederation, states had the right to make their own decisions, and since states' rights were all the rage, there was no provision for a central or national government that would have the right to meddle in the states' affairs.

In fact, it wasn't until the passage of the Constitution in 1789 that a federal government was created.

The absence of a federal government, executive branch, or chief executive in the Articles of Confederation was no accident. It was all part of the plan: After all, the authors of the Articles were rebelling against the tyrannical and upper-handed rule of the king of England, so why would they create a new government that gave someone else the power to control their lives?

Unfortunately for John Hanson, this little glitch in our constitutional law has made it possible for some historians to say he was merely the president of the Continental Congress and not of the United States of America.

CONFUSED?

Here's a quick timeline of history that will make things a lot clearer . . . since you probably only heard a fraction of this in your high school civics class:

- June 11, 1776: The Articles of Confederation, which proposed that the original thirteen colonies form a loose federal government, were presented to the young Continental Congress.
- November 15, 1777: Congress ratified the Articles, but they were still not the law. That wouldn't happen until all thirteen colonies approved.
- 1777-81: Conflict! The citizens of Maryland felt that because the size of their territory was dwarfed by the sizes of Virginia and New York, they wouldn't get equal representation under the Articles of Confederation unless the two larger states ceded some of their land—thus giving Maryland equal footing in terms of size and representation.
- 1781: Finally! All thirteen colonies have signed the Articles of Confederation.

- November 5, 1781: John Hanson was elected "President of the United States in Congress Assembled" by a unanimous vote of Congress.
- 1787: The Constitution was drafted; it was ratified in 1788 and took effect in 1789.
- February 4, 1789: George Washington was the eighth man to be elected president by a unanimous vote of the electoral college.

APPENDIX C: THE GEORGE WASHINGTON CONSPIRACY

"... POWERS AND DUTIES, UNIMAGINABLE TO THE FOUNDERS"

If it's fair to deny that John Hanson was our first president, then it's also fair to say most of the other men we recognize as having served as president (all those, say, from Washington to McKinley) weren't either. For as Edward S. Greenberg and Benjamin I. Page explain in their textbook *The Struggle for Democracy:*

> Since Franklin Roosevelt's day, the American presidency has involved powers and duties, unimaginable to the Founders.

Over time the presidency has evolved. As chief executive, George Washington never had to worry about terrorism, nuclear disarmament, pollution, overpopulation, homelessness, or Internet pornography, or a host of things that must drive modern presidents mad. Was he any less of a president because of it?

JOHN HANSON: WAS HE . . . OR WASN'T HE?

So, WHO ARE you going to believe? Some history professor who wears tweed, smokes a pipe, and gets paid to put college freshmen to sleep? Or are you going to put your money on a couple of guys who were actually there?

"Mr. President, I feel very sensibly the favorable declaration of Congress expressed by your Excellency."

—George Washington to John Hanson, a few weeks after Hanson was elected president

"[George] Washington accepts every condition, law, rule and authority, under the Great Seal and the first President of the United States, John Hanson."

—Thomas Jefferson, while serving as George Washington's secretary of state

APPENDIX C: THE GEORGE WASHINGTON CONSPIRACY

CONSPIRACY THEORISTS WANTED: PLEASE APPLY WITHIN

Here's the thing about John Hanson's tenure in office that is impossible to fathom: If George Washington and Thomas Jefferson knew John Hanson was the first president of the United States, how come the rest of us have never heard of him before?

Could it be . . . a conspiracy?

In 1932 Seymour Wemyss Smith wrote a book called *John Hanson, Our First President.* In the preface Hal F. Lee reported that:

> The only references to John Hanson in the card indices of the New York Public Library mention two articles [both of which Smith wrote] . . . and the *Encyclopaedia Britannica* took cognizance of Hanson for the first time in its Fourteenth Edition, dated 1929, having failed even to mention his name in former editions. . . . To George Washington seven pages of the Encyclopedia are justly devoted—to John Hanson but fourteen brief lines.

Furthermore, Lee writes:

> Washington was a prolific writer. For a score of years he made almost daily entries in his diary. It is odd that Washington's diary is so complete up to the date of the election of John Hanson as our first President, Nov. 5, 1781, and that no further entries can be found until almost a year after Hanson's death. Washington knew Hanson well. It is probable that he commented at length upon Hanson's administration. But his diary covering this period is missing.

326

What Do You Think?

Okay, it's true. Lee sounds a bit like a nut. We thought so too—until we cracked open a copy of *Encyclopaedia Britannica*'s 1954 Great Books series to read the Articles of Confederation verbatim. Everything looked fine until we got to the end . . . where you would expect to see the names of the forty-eight men—which included the likes of Hanson, of course, Samuel Adams, and John Hancock—who signed the Articles into law. Instead we found just one name printed there: George Washington.

George, however, was not one of the forty-eight who signed the Articles of Confederation.

WHITE HOUSE: CONFIDENTIAL

OR WAS JOHN HANSON JUST TOO DARN BORING?

If only John Hanson had lived long enough to read this book. He would have known: It's not what you do as president that counts—it's how much entertainment you provide and how much coverage in the press you get.

As Seymour Wemyss saw it:

> Legends concerning Washington became national epics. He was not only "father of his country." He chopped down a cherry tree and could not tell a lie. He threw a dollar across the Potomac. He was "first in war, first in peace and first in the hearts of his countrymen." Of such stories are heroes made. Did John Hanson lack an efficient publicity department? Was he too absorbed in his job to think of what we today call "public relations"?

Yup. Too absorbed.

And it's kind of sad too. Because even though he was a terrible president when it came to doing things to ensure his immortality and his place in history, when it was time to take care of the unimportant stuff—like running the country—Hanson did an admirable job. Especially when you consider that, according to the Articles of Confederation, he was limited to a term of just one year.

APPENDIX C: THE GEORGE WASHINGTON CONSPIRACY

A YEAR IN THE LIFE OF
OUR FIRST PRESIDENT

JOHN HANSON TOOK office just as the Revolutionary War ended, and he ordered all foreign troops off U.S. soil—making it the first time in almost two hundred years that all thirteen colonies were free of foreign armies. He took the United States from a wartime nation following the Revolutionary War to a nation at peace. This meant that he had to drastically reduce the size of the U.S. Army without causing a mutiny, a difficult task considering that the new government had no money to pay existing soldiers for the work they had already done.

When those same unpaid soldiers threatened to take over the new government by force, every single member of the Continental Congress left . . . except Hanson. Instead he stood tall, and as the lone representative of the new United States government, he negotiated a peaceful settlement.

He created the Treasury Department, the Department of Foreign Affairs, and the position of secretary of war. He also chartered a national bank, initiated a postal service, and established the first consular service. He was even, by some accounts, the one to declare the fourth Thursday of every November a national holiday: Thanksgiving.

POOR JOHN HANSON—ALL THE WORK, NONE OF THE GLORY

WHILE WRITING THIS, your authors found themselves feeling kind of bad for John Hanson.

So bad, in fact, that as soon as we're finished here we're going to write to both our representatives in Congress and the president and demand that John Hanson be recognized and given his due. If you're smart, you'll do the same. After all, if we work together and successfully convince our leaders in Washington to pass a law that says schools must teach about the "real" first president of the United States—in addition to whatever they already have to say about George Washington—we'll all accrue great benefit from our efforts.

First, we'll get the joy and satisfaction of seeing our government at work. Second, we'll each get an opportunity to experience the thrill of knowing our voices count.

And finally, there's the most important reason we should join together and undertake this important project: If we're successful, we'll all get another day off from work every year. After all, we're not going to be foolish enough to insist that the federal government crown this guy as "first president of the United States" without also insisting that they make his birthday (April 3) a national holiday too.

BUT WAIT A MINUTE!

ASTUTE READERS MAY have noticed that in spite of all that has been said here about John Hanson, he probably wasn't the first president of the United States either . . . since the Declaration of Independence was signed in 1776 and Hanson didn't take office until 1781.

So who was in charge before Hanson? For the answer to that question and many others that are sure to arise, we direct you to *The Patriot's Handbook* by Dr. George Grant. Even more a purist than the two of us, Grant says we had a president as early as 1774, when the Continental Congress first began to meet. Grant's list of presidents, therefore, begins with Peyton Randolph of Virginia.

Randolph served as the president of the first Continental Congress from September 5 to October 21, 1774. But while Grant presents a convincing case for Randolph's presidency, Hanson still gets our vote. After all, you'll recall Hanson was the guy Washington called "Mr. President" and whom Jefferson called "the first President of the United States." And how can you argue with that?

ACKNOWLEDGMENTS

One cold winter night in 1995 I took my girlfriend Jody to the movies to see a schmaltzy love story called *The American President*. At the end of the show, two very significant events occurred. First, as the credits rolled I had the idea for this book. Second, as I got up to leave, Jody pulled me back down into my seat, kissed me, and asked me—a solidly confirmed thirty-four-year-old bachelor—if I wouldn't like to be her husband someday.

As good an idea as I thought this book was, I thought Jody's idea was even better. And I'm no longer a bachelor, solidly confirmed or otherwise. Meanwhile, I'm happy to report that this book—and everything else in my life—is demonstrably better for the addition of the ever-smiling, ever-loving Jody Stebben.

I am fortunate to have many others in my life who offer support and encouragement, including my new South Carolina friends Laurie and Tim Clarke, Mary and Max Sherman, Vince Perna, Polly and Mark Weiss, Steve and Laurie Berman, Marcy Rosenthal and her hubby Ron, Pat and Barb Harrington, Rick and Lynn Holgate, and Snow Phillip, Louis Youhasz and Fred Wszolek, Aimee Ratner, and a great chiropractor and friend Dr. Chris Benoit. All the members of the great world-beat/southern funk/melodic rock bank SOL DRIVEN TRAIN kept me in tune while writing . . . and of course, Jill Bradley in Nashville kept me on track. Also great Monterey friends like Paulette Lynch and Ken Peterson, Amanda and Jeff Holder, Drs. Cynthia and Richard Westbrook, Leticia Medina and Don Kohrs, Mike and Hilary and Matthew and Callie Sutton. And I am indebted to two brilliant business guys named Ted Hoffman and Mark Andersen. I also owe a huge smile and thanks to my most-trusted dentist, Dr. Daniel J. Turner, and my very good friend and accountant, Jim Jorgensen. Also my friends David Friend and Swami Kumaresan at Carbonite.com, Kim and Carla Garretson, Kelly Rodriques, and my Mount Kilimanjaro buddies Charles Hamilton, Tomasz Nadrowski, Alex Sturminger and Deborah Arenstein deserve many many thanks. And as always, I owe great thanks to Denis Boyles.

My friends in the radio world have been equally supportive (even when they didn't know it), including: Pat Farnack at WCBS in New York; Mike Jakaitis and Adrienne Mitchell at WTOP in Washington D.C.; Linda Blake and Chris Finch at *The Leeza Gibbons Show;* Bob Klopfenstein at *DOUG STEPHAN'S GOOD DAY*; Shelli Gonshorowski at *The Lisa Birnbach Show;* Shana Pearlman at *FOX Across America;* Matt and Ramona and Brent at *The Matt and Ramona Show;* Jim Scott, Rich Walburg, and Russ Jackson at WLW in Cincinnati; Brandon Webster in Salt Lake City; Gary Allen, John Matlak, Mary Kronkowski, and Phil Tower at WOOD Radio in Grand Rapids; Enoch Perry, John Zimney, and Charlie Butcher at WOWO in Fort Wayne; Mark Shiver and Kevin Miller at WPTF in Raleigh; Mike Miller, Dave Woodward, and Renee Scott at WIMA in Lima; and my buddy Michael Cooper.

And I owe many thanks to the following friends in the magazine and publishing world: Robin Shallow, Karen Mazzotta, Sheryl Spain, Jon Hammond, Allison Falkenberry, Fredricka Brookfield, Angelica De Las Salas, Cathy Facchiano, Natalie Ramos, Peter Moore, Bill Stieg, Matt Marion, Matt Bean, Erin Hobday, Seth Porges, Denise Foley, Marianne McGinnis, Jeff Csatari, Trevor Thieme, Rob Gerth, Kate Dailey, Cristina Goyanes, Deanna Michalopoulos, Bob Brody, Lou Schuler, and Lissa Brown. And, of course, a heap of thanks go to Dave Zinczenko at *Men's Health* magazine, Jennifer Cook at *Prevention* magazine, Stephen Perrine at *Best Life* magazine, and Kristina Johnson at *Women's Health* magazine for letting me bring my radio firepower to each of their magazines. And of course, I cannot forget to thank my agent Laurie Harper and my friends Ron Pitkin, Mary Sanford, and Danielle Edwards at Cumberland House Publishing.

We are grateful to Senator John McCain and Congressman Joseph Crowley, along with Elizabeth McWhorter, Christopher S. McCannell, and Shawn Hodjati from their respective offices.

And finally, there is my family to thank: my brother, Marty Stebben and all the other Stebbenses (Earle, Sharalyne, Jef and SaDawna and Annikah, Matt and Ora [and their kids]); the Zuckers (Stephanie and Rebekkah and Roni, Felix and Michael and Shana, Steve and Lori); the Manns (Linda, Cheryl and Sharon, David and Kelly and their kids, and Darren and Dena and Ashley); Mira M. White, Mike Leifer, Bill and Maggie Armstrong, Jackie Diamond, Mike and Rosemary Tobin, Sheri Tobin, and Fred Fishel.

Finally, darn it, I've got to thank Rob Reiner, Michael Douglas, and Annette Bening for making that sappy little movie *The American President*. As silly as this may sound, things just haven't been the same around here since I saw it.

—G. S.

I've got a very special "thanks" to extend to one particular United States president . . . but I'll save that for last.

And as much as I appreciate and respect the American presidency, I must first acknowledge lots of other people: people who have impacted my life and continue to do so in ways that the president simply could not. (Unless, of course, I was related to one . . . for more on this, see the chapter called "Executive Privledge[s]!").

Several people enabled me to take on this endeavor and to complete it. First, to my wife Nell Dunivent-Hill: Thank you for your support as I was researching and writing. More importantly, thank you for "believing"—even when I did not. To my son Graham Hill: Thank you for the richness you contribute to my life. You know that I love my work, but the best job I get to do every day is to be your dad. To my coauthor Gregg Stebben: Thank you for your friendship over these many years, and for inviting me to collaborate with you on this project; the best is still to come! To my friend and life mentor Bob Shank: Thanks for your wisdom and guidance that has helped to bring me here. To my friend and attorney (and the Mayor of Tempe, Arizona) Hugh Hallman, and his lovely wife (and the First Lady of Tempe) Dr. Susan Hallman: Thank you for your leadership. You are both "White House material," if ya know what I'm sayin' (could happen). To Laurie Harper: Thank you for being the "most excellent" literary agent, and overseeing this project. To Ron Pitkin, Danielle Edwards, and Mary Sanford of Cumberland House Publishing: Thank

ACKNOWLEDGMENTS

you for having the "vision" for this project, and for the opportunity to do business with you. To "the God-Parents," Brad and Julie Hahn: now that the book has been released, would one of you please propose a toast? (Brad?) To Chris Bowen of Direct Clarity Dot Com: Thank you for helping me navigate "the Web," and navigate "the changes"—and yes, "the changes" have been for the better. To Charley Coppinger: Thank you for being a wise friend on the journey—always. To Senator John McCain, my Senior Senator from Arizona: Thank you for lending your remarks to this project, and more importantly, thank you for your service to our great nation. And to Ernie Brown: When Governor Bush nicknamed you "Big E," it wasn't just about your height—it was about the person you are. Thank you for being that person.

But wait, there's more! Every author has a roster of people who have helped make him who he is. A big thanks to: Todd Minturn, Pam Rice, Dave and Diane Bower (distant relatives of Jack), Fred and Sally Baker, Bryan Duncan, Jeanette Betts, Rick Erickson, Tony and Bobbie Valente, Chris Bassett, Dave and Amy Blazak, Dave Stoop, Debbie Betts, Ron and Tami Baily, Dr. Scott Rae, Dr. Richard Rawls, Dan Labounty, Pat Plannette, Ken Metcalf, Paul and Diane Patterson, David Smith, Cheryl and Mickey Nation, Michael Brown, Edwin Farnsworth, Allen Natella, Robert Lovell, Dr. Bill Dyment, Gordon Fake, Dr. Steven Gustaveson, Jim Beattie, Andy Biggs, Doreen Hill, Dr. Bill Maier, Nicole Perry, Summer Yim, Tino Salvaje, Vernon Parker, Brett Scott, Ray Perry, Randy Stonehill, Brent Larsen, Michael Bazyler Esq., Srgnt. Dave Hill, Kent Forde, Mark Anderson, Norma Mendoza, Kevin Baker Esq., Mike and Kimberly Kupanoff, Bill Purcell, Trif and Peggy Kupanoff, Barbara X. White, Ben Hubbard, Amanda Williams, Steve and Ja Betts, Glenn Fuller, Patricia Kempthorne, Michael Mears, Stan Hill, Kent Rini, Kevin and Laura Rice, Ronald Lerma, John and Betsy Kaiser, Gene Hill, Matt and Kim McMahon, Mike Churchin, Judy Redmond, Kenman Wong, Keith Watts, Nathan Sproul, and Juan and Lois Ibarra.

And what about "the biz?" Yes, I have known some incredible people as I have traveled along my life's journey through this insane and wonderful business that we call "the media." I owe thanks to so many, in no particular order: Guy Paul Hackman, John Timm,

Ruth Michaels, Tom Liddy, Haagan Higgins, Larry Elder, Jim Meyers, Joe Davis, Gary Owens, Mariam Stepanian, Jim Seemiller, Amy Bolton, Dave Armstrong, Robin Bertolucci, Woody Woodhull, Jim Bohannon, Ed Atsinger, Carey Edwards, Jessica Sherman, Tim & Willy, Dave Hermann, Roger Marsh, Carrie Wilson, David "Mosky" Moskowitz, Brenda K. Brown, Jim Sharp, David R. Perez, Al Summers, Marina Wilson, Sydney Hay, Chris Lavoie, Karen Lyndsay, Dave Pratt, Cara Liu, Steven Gregory, Stephanie Miller, Ted Houston, Dan Hay, Katie Raml, Hugh Hewitt, Alan Sledge, Trent Franks, Andi Barness, David Yurisarri, Becky Lynn, Jeff & Jer, James Grisham, Deb Greenbaum, Michael Anthony, JD Freeman, Jen Yantz, George W. Tanner, Dawn McCauley, Danny Romero, Robin Marshall, Mike Patrick, Kaley O'Kelley, Bart Graves, Susan Karis, Tom Brown, Laurie Cantillo, Scooter Sherwood, Sylvia Aimerito, Mark Talercio, Lee Logan, Nancy Abramson, Jason Christopher, Bill Doyle, Gary Campbell, Blanquita Cullum, Phil Jenrich, Steve Ludwig, Robin Anderson, Brian Perez, the late Barbara Olson (09-11-01), Rudy Grande, Steve Carr, Michael Cooper, Andrew Babinski, Robert Robb, Carey Pena, Eric Hogue, Dan Godzich, Cruella-Michella-Buffy-Lee Larson, Clark Judge, Jackie Mahaney, Mark Wallengren, Eric Zott, John Broeske, Sean Hannity, Kim Ketchel, Frank Pastore, Melodie Burkett, Jim Hodson, JD Hayworth, Mike Perkins, Jan D'Atri, Mike Gallagher, Angie Handa, R. J. Curtis, Vicki Fiorelli, Fred Missman, Chris Core, Tonya Campos, Rich Galen, "The Nearly Famous Barry Young," Tyler Cox, Michael Harrison, Jerry Klein, Mark Jeffrey, Laura Ingraham, Tony Evans, Lee Habib, Greg Moceri, Ellen Ratner, Scott Hogensen, Laurie Larsen, Scott Fisher, Mike Watkiss, Barbeth Pinkney, Steve Bridges, Mark Larson, Kristin Jekel, Preston Westmoreland, Mike Conner, Christine Ferguson, Steve Hosher, Shawn Parr, Hillary Hallows, Tony Snow, Tom Tradup, Patrick Lancaster, Ron Hartenbaum, Heidi Foglesong, Gary Lycan, Jason Barry, John Sebastian, Kim Komando, Don Barrett, C. J. Cowie, Mark Masters, Darrin Cameron, Kristi Tedesco, Jeffrey Davis, Eric Zott, Farrell Quinlan, Christine Jones, John Hook, Bobby Volare, Kay Poland, Craig Whitney, Royal Norman, Elizabeth McWhorter, John Rubal, Tisa LaSorte, Trevor Oliver, Darrin Miiler, Frank DiBignara, Blair Garner, John Corken, Jennifer Cooke, Mike Jaworski, Michael Medved, Captain Rod Harris, Katie Moore, Mark Scoon, Brenda

ACKNOWLEDGMENTS

Vance, Joe Crummey, Dave "Erv" Ervin, Tori Ueltschi, Bruce Jacobs, Rebecca Hagelin, Barry Besse, Ray Lopez, Paul Duckworth, Renee Thomas, Dr. Bob Martin, Roberta Gale, Bo Reynolds, Matt Drudge, Ron Gerson, Gary Schonfeld, Gary Harper, Lee Hill, Kevin Nitsche, Al Peterson, Rachel Van Hofwegen, Doug Steffan, Shana Pearlman, Tom Morine, Jeff Conaway, John Quinlan, Jessica Storz, Bob Coburn, Terri Gilberg, Bob McClay, Connie Powell, Ray Appleton, Phil Gordon, Scott Rummell, and Brad Gould.

And finally, a special thanks to President Gerald Ford, the first president to shake my hand. It was 1976, and you, Mr. President, were campaigning for a second term in office, although in reality you were seeking reelection to your own, first "full term" as president (see page 318). I was a twelve-year-old kid, thrilled that my father had taken me to see the president of the United States—appearing at Mile Square Park in Fountain Valley, California. Thank you, President Ford, for serving our country at a very difficult time in its history, and for shaking the hand of a kid who managed to squeeze an arm past the Secret Service agents.

And by the way, Mr. President . . . I was NOT that kid in the crowd holding the "Carter/Mondale" sign (but you never know . . . that smart-aleck kid might have been my coauthor, Gregg Stebben).

—A. H.